Paddy Finn's Children

The author, 1960

T. V. Glover

Paddy Finn's Children

The Pentland Press Ltd.
Edinburgh Cambridge Durham

First published in 1992 by
The Pentland Press Ltd.
Brockerscliffe
Witton le Wear
Durham

ISBN 1 872795 35 8

Typeset, printed and bound by Polyprint
48 Pleasance
Edinburgh EH8 9TJ

Contents

List of Illustrations

Foreword

I am happy to introduce Terry Glover's History of the Finns, though there is little more to add. Perhaps I should point out my respect for all the work he has done, in providing a gift to his descendants and to us "collateral" relatives. He has done an especially good job, I think, of portraying people in the past as real live people, whose lives it is a pleasure to share over the remote reach of time. His enthusiasm and energy for the task has certainly been an inspiration to me to keep plugging away to find new information. A family search is so much more fun when there are others eager to share each new discovery. Terry's extra research into the pubs of Manchester is doubtless worthy of special commendation, as has been his objectivity in uncovering new trails even when they led in startling directions!

It is a source of continuous amazement to me that, before we began our mutual search into the family history, neither of us knew the other existed. Terry had grown up in England and worked in Africa; I had grown up in Aruba and worked in the US. Then Florence Hughes and Cissie Harman brought us together by letter across the ocean, and in no time at all we had developed a working relationship that took us walking together, with Ida and Sue, up Main Street in Sarcoxie to the old Barney Finn homestead, and into Altrincham Cemetery to see where Kate Finn Glover is buried. By now I feel a kinship towards him as a brother, though I'm sure it's more from shared interest in the family than from genes.

I'm delighted to hear that Terry is printing his book in more permanent form, and hope that will make it possible for many other readers to share it.

Bill Moyer

Irish Beginnings

They say it was the Lord Protector who drove the Finns from the rich pastures of central Ireland into the wilds of Connaught. That may be so, for under the Cromwellian Act of Settlement the English annexed a further nine counties to meet arrears in army pay, and many dispossessed Irish families took refuge in the few remaining unpossessed counties of Mayo, Roscommon, Galway and Clare. There they eked out a frugal existence under the rule of the Commonwealth, the restoration and fall of the House of Stuart, and suffered the following hundred years of Penal Law that forbade them, among other things, to exercise their religion, to own land or possess a horse worth more than five pounds in value.

Whatever their origins, they were certainly there in the last decade of the eighteenth century when Jack Finn was born. He grew up to be a farmer in Cloontia on the eastern border of County Mayo.

His farm stands to this day by a small stream, a mile or so east of the Cloontia crossroads. It is a stone building with outhouses at either end pointing north-east in the direction of the distant limestone hill of Kesh Corran in the neighbouring county of Sligo. In the centre of the main building the wall projects about two feet, making an alcove in the living-room to house the bed in which he and his wife slept.

Jack married a girl named Catherine Kane, who came from a few miles over the County Sligo border. She bore him several sons, the seventh of whom was Paddy, the Finn who took his children across the Irish Sea to live in Manchester.

About the time of the great potato famine of 1846, Jack Finn left his farm in Cloontia and took his family across the border into the area of County Sligo where Catherine's kinsfolk lived. The reason is not apparent, but it could be that the farm was too small to support his growing family, or that one of his wife's brothers had told them of a farm falling vacant in the area and that there would be more opportunity for their sons to find employment there.

The journey into County Sligo followed the course of the Owenmore river, and the farm he leased was by its bank, where the river turned eastward below the hill of Clooneen. That was to be his home until the day he died.

One by one Jack Finn's sons married and settled as farmers in the neighbourhood. Michael, his eldest son, who was born about 1820, farmed at Ragwood a mile or two south of Clooneen, possibly working for one of his mother's brothers who farmed there. At Ragwood he met and married Kitty Radican. He leased a farm with ten acres of land to which his father-in-law added a further seven acres of leasehold land as a dowry.

Jack's seventh son, Paddy, married Mary Hannon and leased a twenty-six-acre farm by the banks of the Owenmore on the other side of the hill from his parents. He and his father later acquired a further ten acres of bogland between them.

Paddy's farm is still standing. It is reached by a path off the road from Gorteen to Ballymote, just north of Gorteen. The path slopes gently down for about a quarter of a mile to the farm. The farm buildings are quite small. The larger one, running from north to south, is about twenty feet long and ten feet wide with white, plastered, stone walls. About twenty feet to the east there is a small stone building about fifteen feet by ten standing at right angles to it. The buildings are connected by a flat-roofed shed, walled at the back but open at the front. Today the shed houses cattle, but in Paddy's time the main living-room of the farm was located in this demolished area.

To the north of the farm the land slopes downward to a drainage ditch about five feet wide and deep. To the south-east the Owenmore curves across the meadows that gave Clooneen its name. Behind the farm the Clooneen hill rises rather steeply. The front of the farm looks across the valley of Clooneen to Riversdale Hill, which has two raths on its summit. The raths are ancient earthen forts, circular in shape and about thirty feet in diameter. Their walls are now broken and patched with new earth and rock. There are thorn trees growing around them, and blackberries, whitethorn and haws grow on the hill slopes.

Paddy and Mary's first child was born at the farm in 1854, a son named John after Paddy's father. Their next two children were boys, Michael and Tom. In 1861 their first daughter was born. She was christened Catherine after Paddy's mother, but was known as Kate. After Kate there were four more sons, Patrick, James,

Edward and Bernard, the seventh son of a seventh son, born on 7th March 1869. The family was completed on the first of June 1872 with the birth of twin girls, Roseanne and Maria, affectionately known as Molly.

The world of Paddy's children was small and sparsely populated. Their immediate neighbours lived in a rented labourer's cottage on Paddy's land. The labourer, Martin Millmow, was a poor, hunch-backed, feeble man with watery eyes. He was looked after by his daughter Mary. To the children her main housekeeping duty seemed to be standing over the peat fire cooking porridge, which she was always ready to share with any hungry young Finn who passed by.

Martin was a gifted storyteller, and he regaled the children with tales of Irish grandeur in far gone days when "her Kings with banners of green unfurled led the Red Branch Knights to danger".

He told them legends of the hill of Kesh Corran, named after gentle Corran the harpist, and how in its caves the great Irish king, Cormac MacArt, was suckled by a she-wolf. Cormac was the grandson of Conn of the Hundred Battles, who gave Connaught its name.

Among Martin's tales of more recent times the one that appealed to Paddy's son James the most were the verses about Seamus O'Brien, mainly because they both bore the same Christian name. Seamus, a fugitive from the 1798 uprising, spent many cold nights in hiding on a bleak mountainside before being captured and sentenced to death by public hanging. He mounted the gallows accompanied by a priest who, as they prayed together, managed to cut the condemned man's bonds. The sympathetic onlookers pressed forward excitedly and carried him away to safety.

> The soldiers ran this way, the policemen ran that,
> And Father Malone lost his best Sunday hat.

The chase was on again, but it was too late.

> He has boarded a ship, and soon he will be
> In America, darling, the land of the free.

Martin's stories were not entirely confined to national history and legend. He told his young listeners how the Finns came to Clooneen. It began with the defeat of the Spanish Armada when the English fleet chased the surviving ships eastward down the English Channel. The Spanish admiral planned to circumnavigate the British

3

Isles to gain access to the Atlantic and the home ports of Spain, but he met with high winds and rough seas and many ships were wrecked off the coasts of Scotland and Ireland. One galleon was smashed to pieces on the rocks off Yona. The captain-general managed to get ashore and was befriended by the people of Sligo. He settled in Ireland to farm the land, and it was through him the Finns of Clooneen were descended.

The children were thrilled to hear that their ancestor was a Spanish grandee. That would account for their dark hair. For their family could not have common ancestry with the rest of the Finns whose surname came from the Irish *fionn*, meaning fair-haired.

Martin became the children's friend and comforter. He would take them mushroom-picking in the meadows, he would lift them high up to the eaves of the barn to see a swallow sitting on its nest of eggs, and he would take them fishing on the banks of the Owenmore. It was he who had baited young Bernard's hook with a worm when Bernard had caught his first fish, a small perch, which he rushed home to exhibit, cook and eat with great relish.

The centre of family life on Paddy's farm was in the living-room, now demolished. It had a wide, stone fireplace in which a peat fire burned day and night. An iron crane was fixed in one side of the fireplace with a large pot suspended from it that could readily be swung over the fire to cook the meals. The family diet consisted of oatmeal porridge, buttermilk, eggs, potatoes, cabbage and bacon; and occasionally fish from Sligo Bay, with oysters as a special treat. Anything left uneaten on plate or in pot would be taken by Mary to feed her chickens. Above the fireplace, tarnished by the smoke, was a picture of St. Patrick.

On many an evening, when their day's work was done, neighbouring relatives and friends would gather around Paddy's fireplace in the mellow light of the oil lamps and smoke their clay pipes whilst they talked over the local news and gossip. The children looked on as interested spectators, particularly fascinated by the accuracy with which their uncle, Brian Hannon, could spit a distance through clenched teeth into the glowing peat, an ability he had no doubt gotten through years of tobacco chewing.

Paddy was a hospitable man, and it would not be long before the poteen was passed round, rebel songs were sung, and the talk and laughter grew louder and coarser. Mary was a quiet, sweet-natured woman and on these occasions she would nod to Kate and make her excuses while she and Kate rounded up the younger children and took them to bed.

There would be a momentary hush in the living-room, broken by the solo voice of somebody singing a quieter rebel song, perhaps the air set to Tom Moore's verse telling of the loved one of Robert Emmet, the young Irish patriot who was executed for treason in 1803.

> *She is far from the land where her young hero sleeps,*
> *And lovers around her are sighing,*
> *But coldly she turns from their gazes and weeps,*
> *For her heart in the cold grave is lying.*

The children would sleep until the morning sun silvered the blanket of cloud above Kesh Corran. The house was still again except for sounds of activity by the cooking pot and the clump of Paddy's boots as he got ready for work. Outside, the silence was broken by the rasp of the corncrake and the plaintive call of the curlew. Below the farm the Owenmore murmured softly as its waters rippled among the green rushes below its banks. Then, as the children dressed for school, the house was filled with a much younger noise of laughter and excitement than it had held the night before.

The children's school was over the brow of a hill, a short way down the road to Ballymote. Carberry's National School was a building some sixty feet long and thirty feet wide that housed a single classroom with a bare earth floor trodden down hard and firm by generations of barefoot pupils. At the upper end of the classroom there was an open fireplace in which a peat fire burned in the winter months. The pupils were expected to provide fuel for the fire, and their place in the classroom depended upon whether they had brought turf to school that day. If they had not, they were sent to the back of the class, far away from the warmth of the fire. Their chief consolation was that they were equally as distant from the headmaster, who sat at his desk on one side of the fireplace with his cane at the ready. On the other side of the fireplace were two grandfather clocks, one in working order and the other with a broken face.

John Carberry, the headmaster who gave the school its name, was also the local registrar of births, marriages and deaths, and as such had an intimate knowledge of the family history of his pupils. He was always neatly dressed in a freshly laundered shirt and bow tie. Three ornamental studs fastened and adorned the shirt front.

The studs were the indirect cause of the mishap to the broken clock. One of three boys who had been banished to the back of the class because they had brought no peat that morning bet that he could hit the middle stud with a small stone fired from the catapult they had smuggled into class. It was a foolish and disastrous wager. He missed his aim completely. There was a shattering noise from the clock, followed by an uneasy silence as the headmaster, unaware that he was the target, called the unknown culprit to step forward. As nobody moved, and nobody was prepared to identify the offender, he gave every boy a caning, including all the Finn brothers who were unfortunate enough to be at school that day.

Paddy fully approved of Mr Carberry's sense of justice, and practised it himself in the firm belief that it were better the innocent suffer than the guilty escape punishment. That was his reasoning after the affair of Uncle Jack's geese.

Each evening, Paddy's brother, Jack Finn, would gather his family around the fireside and they would recite the rosary in Irish. On one particular summer evening the Finn boys, with Bernard trailing in their wake, strolled across the meadows in the direction of their uncle's cottage. As they approached, they noticed Jack's flock of geese in the yard, and through the open doorway they could hear the mumble of the family prayers. Bent on mischief, the boys rounded up the geese and drove them through the doorway, honking and hissing. They then hid on the blind side of the cottage until the geese emerged. After the third intrusion Uncle Jack realised that it was not pure chance, but a human agency that was driving his geese indoors. Struggling from his knees, he hobbled to the door and hurled a torrent of Gaelic abuse after his tormentors as they vanished into the gloom.

Uncle Jack reported the incident to Paddy, who quickly concluded that all his sons should be punished, including young Bernard who, because of his tender years, could have been little more than a spectator to the misdemeanour.

After receiving his spanking, Bernard ran over to Martin Millmow to tell him of his misfortune. Martin comforted him by telling him that one day he would grow up to be the greatest of the Finns, which was a great distinction considering that so far the greatest had been no less than a shipwrecked Spanish grandee.

Then, to amuse him, Martin told him the story of Mike O'Shea and his brother Denis.

Mike and his wife had fallen on such hard times that he was compelled to drive his last cow to Limerick market. The way was long and hard and Mike walked through the night so that he could sell the cow at the morning auction.

By midnight he had reached an old ruined castle, the home of fairies, good and evil. There he encountered a fairy who offered to take the cow in exchange for a bottle. He was to return home, get his wife to put a clean cloth on the table, uncork the bottle and see what happened. He could do this regularly, but only once a day. Then, in a flash, the fairy and the cow disappeared, leaving Mike alone in the dark with the bottle in his hand.

When he got home his wife berated him for losing the cow, but, after much scolding, she agreed that they had nothing to lose by following the fairy's instructions.

Mike took the cork out of the bottle. One by one three gnomes leapt out of the bottle, and each placed a gold piece on the tablecloth before climbing back into the bottle. This happened each day and Mike grew rich.

That might have been the end of the story had it not been for Mike's brother Denis. Curious about the newly won wealth, Denis, by guile and drink, wrested the secret from Mike and persuaded him to sell him the bottle. So Denis became rich and Mike mismanaged his own affairs so much that once again he was compelled to take his last cow to Limerick market, and once again met a fairy by the ruined castle. But this time it was an evil fairy.

The fairy offered a bottle for the cow, and Mike returned home rejoicing in his good fortune. But when the bottle was opened there emerged not three gnomes bearing gold, but three gnomes bearing shillelaghs with which they beat Mike so unmercifully that his wife begged them to stop in the name of the Blessed Trinity. Halted by the pious invocation, the evil trio ceased their beating and crept back into the bottle.

Mike and his wife were in despair until Mike, knowing his brother's insatiable greed, decided they should try to sell Denis the bottle. At first Denis was suspicious, but when they told him he could open the bottle before he paid for it his curiosity and greed got the better of him. Denis uncorked the bottle and out jumped the evil gnomes. They beat him so fiercely that he screamed for mercy. But the beating continued until he consented to give back to Mike the original bottle.

7

So Mike became rich again, but this time he shared his good fortune with Denis, and so both families prospered and became a credit to the community.

Bernard left for home in a much happier state of mind. He made a detour across the meadow and walked back to the farm along the river bank. There he saw his brother Michael standing under the blackthorn tree looking up at the sloes ripening among its branches. Bernard approached with some trepidation, because the tree was out of bounds to him, or at least it had been until recently, when it became known that John and Michael were leaving home to make their way in the world. Its present status was not yet clear.

The blackthorn, which stood on the river bank below the farm, had been Michael's favourite haunt ever since he had been given an old, illicit pinfire revolver. When the Owenmore flooded the meadows, as it often did, the floodwater would spread right up to Mary Finn's garden by the side of the farm, leaving the blackthorn partly submerged to make a perfect blind from which Michael could take pot-shots at the waterfowl. Mary had voiced her fears about the children playing within the range of Michael's shots. Hence the out of bounds order.

Mary's fears were justified when one day, perhaps because the river water was low, Michael, accompanied by his brother Edward, climbed Riversdale hill to shoot from the cover of its raths. The revolver went off accidentally and Edward was nearly shot.

The incident distressed Mary, and Paddy saw to it that the gun remained in its hiding place behind a stone in the fireplace for many a day. To the children the near tragedy was all the more frightening because of its location. They remembered the night when Tom returned home one evening and reported that he had seen a double row of fairy lights among the raths. He may have glimpsed the light of glow-worms in the mating season, but to the children, steeped in Martin Millmow's stories of the distant past, they were the lights of the little people guiding their way to some secret tryst as they did in the bygone days when Maev was queen of Connaught.

Michael's sport ended on the day that the authorities conducted a general search for illicit firearms. The police visited Paddy's farm, and as they entered the living-room the children stood petrified, their gaze fixed on the stone in the fireplace where Michael's gun lay concealed, terrified that their looks would betray the hiding place, yet too hypnotised by the stone to divert their glances elsewhere.

All went well, however. The police completed their search and left the farm empty-handed. If they noticed what fascination the fireplace held for the children they may have attributed it to the cooking pot simmering close by, all ready to provide the young Finns with a much wanted meal.

Neither Michael nor John took part in the affair of Uncle Jack's geese. Their days of juvenile pranks were far behind them, and having obtained little satisfaction and little remuneration from work on neighbouring farms, both decided to leave home.

John took the Queen's shilling and enlisted in the army. After his initial training was completed he was posted overseas to Malta. Michael, in the manner of the poacher turned gamekeeper, chose the Royal Irish Constabulary and left Clooneen for Dublin.

For Mary, the departure of her two eldest sons was offset by the pleasure of her baby twin daughters. They were the last occupants of the family cradle, one lying at each end vigorously pulling on a feeding bottle. By the time they had outgrown the cradle Tom and Kate had left school. Tom helped his father on the farm and Kate helped full time in the many household duties.

The cradle met its end by Tom, Patrick, James and Edward carrying it ceremoniously out of the house and dumping it in the Owenmore as a demonstration against impoverishing Finn fecundity. Bernard watched the procession with mixed feelings. He recalled several incidents that led him to believe that he too had not been a wholly welcome addition to an already large family, but he took comfort in Martin Millmow's prophecy that one day he would the greatest of all the Finns, and in the gifts bestowed on him as a seventh son of a seventh son.

By Gaelic tradition the seventh son is endowed with natural gifts including, in some degree, the power of healing. Bernard began to enjoy exercising that power from an early age, mainly because it raised him to a level of importance no ordinary childish talent could achieve. Each Sunday morning, when Mass had ended, he propped a one-legged milk stool against the pig sty and sat there awaiting the arrival of any sufferer of ringworm, warts, hives, boils or kindred ailment. His practice soon got known, and neighbouring friends and relatives calling upon Mary and Paddy would stop by the pig sty to have their ailment treated.

Bernard began his treatment by piping out a Hail Mary. Then he would lay his right hand on the afflicted part, and conclude with a

9

Paternoster or two. Tradition forbade a seventh son from exercising his powers for monetary gain, but if the odd copper were thrust in his hand Bernard did not disdain the token of gratitude.

With Tom helping on the farm, Paddy expanded his work by acting as drayman to a licensed victualler named Flannery. The business was in Ballaghaderreen, south of Gorteen, and Paddy's deliveries would take him into the neighbouring county of Roscommon. There were tales to tell of the world outside Clooneen. One day Paddy saw a man at the Gorteen crossroads mounting a penny-farthing bicycle. "The fellow hopped on a big wheel and went like the wind," he told his amazed family. And the incident was retold again and again around the fireside when the drink flowed.

Sometimes Tom would accompany him on his deliveries in Roscommon. One evening they were returning home through Frenchpark past the estate of Lord de Freyne, whose owner had been hanged in effigy outside the main door of his mansion by his tenants and labourers during the great potato famine. As they drove along the road by the estate, Paddy on the seat of the draycart and Tom astride Old Charlie the horse, a man, hidden in the hedgerow, fired a gun at them. Paddy received a charge of shot. Old Charlie shied and threw Tom, breaking his arm. Their unknown assailant ran off into the night. Who he was or why he fired at them they never knew. He was not caught. They drove home as best they could. Their arrival was met with relief by Mary, who was worried by their lateness, and then by distress at their condition. It was another story for the fireside, but it was some time before they could ride through Frenchpark at ease.

On 5th October 1875, old Jack Finn died of cancer at his farm on the other side of the hill. There was much coming and going in Clooneen as the Finn clan converged there for the wake. From Ragwood came Jack's eldest son Michael with his grown-up sons, Michael, Edward and Thomas. From the north-west of Clooneen came Jack's sons Thomas of Kiltycreen and James of Kilshavy. It was James who reported his father's death and took his family to live with his widowed mother on Jack's farm. From across the meadows on the other side of the Owenmore came John from Cloonanure, the Uncle Jack of the geese incident, and from down the lane came Paddy's youngest brother, Dominic.

Other Finns and Kanes gathered round Paddy's fireside throughout the wake, most of them related to Jack or Catherine. But whoever they were, or from whence they came, all were welcome, and the drink flowed freely.

The year after Jack's death a great fever epidemic swept across Ireland. From Dublin Paddy received notification that his son, Police Constable Michael Finn, had died of typhus. The epidemic reached Clooneen, and young Bernard became its first victim. He lay in his bed dangerously ill. In his delerium he saw a single file of black demons approach the bed. Their white eyes rolled as they came nearer, and each brandished a long club. Every time he screamed they vanished, only to return again and again. In one period of calm he heard a voice whisper, "Poor little fellow, he can't recover." Then he drifted into a carefree, peaceful world of neither fear nor worry. When consciousness returned the crisis had passed and he slowly began to recover.

In Malta, John contracted Malta fever, an undulant fever transmitted in the bacteria of infected animals and commonly got through drinking goat's milk. The fever, which often proved fatal, undulates for two or three weeks. It then may subside for a time, but can recur and persist for several months.

John recovered from the initial bout of fever, but his condition was sufficiently grave for him to be invalided home. He returned to Clooneen on sick leave but, perhaps because of Bernard's illness, he went over to his uncle Michael's farm to recuperate. Whilst he was there he had another bout. John died at Ragwood on 22nd September 1876. The cause of death was given as three-week fever, possibly to indicate a recurrence of Malta fever rather than the local fever endemic at that time. He was only twenty-two years old, a year older than his brother Michael.

That autumn the fever epidemic struck the Finn family again. This time Mary was the victim. The household was devastated. In some ways John and Michael had been lost to them when they had enlisted. Now the family had been struck at its very heart. Kate, now fifteen, nursed her mother as best she could and did most of the arduous housework. Paddy and Tom moved in and out of the house like ghosts of their former selves. Kate's younger brothers went off to school fearful of what each day might bring. Only the four-year-old twins were spared the constant worry of their mother's illness, although they too were uneasily aware of the anxiety that pervaded the household. Mary well was the sweet, comforting harbour when the sea of life was troubled. Now that Mary was sick there remained only the cold, comfortless sea. Kate knew in her heart that she would have to provide that harbour, now so sorely missed.

One day during his mother's illness Edward was fishing by the river when he heard women wailing in the meadows. A Mr Finn had drowned off Rosses Point, north-west of the town of Sligo, and was being brought home for burial. Edward never discovered who the drowned man was, or whether he was a relative who may have attended his grandfather's wake the year before. The thought passed through his mind that the sea had claimed a Finn as recompense for the Finn who escaped its clutches when the Spanish galleon was wrecked all those years ago.

The fourth of December began like any other day of Mary's illness. Kate, after a broken night's sleep, was up early preparing the family breakfast. Her father and Tom went out to cut peat in the nearby bogland. Her younger brothers made their way to school. The twins dawdled at the table and amused themselves while Kate went and attended to her mother.

Paddy and Tom found it cold and miserable that morning as they squelched in the peat bog cutting and stacking the turf. The mossy ground was waterlogged and a ditch of water had formed along the straight bank of hewn peat. Father and son worked quietly and moodily in the wet and cold. They spoke little. Each was a prisoner of his own thoughts.

Their work was interrupted by Kate's cry from the farmyard. "Dada, Tom. Quick."

They hurried back to the farm, but when they reached the house Mary was dead.

Tom took the draycart to inform the doctor and then called at the school. There were tears in John Carberry's eyes as he approached each of the brothers in turn and told them that their mother had died and that they could go home. He walked slowly back to his desk by the fireside and announced, as if by an afterthought, that school was over for the day. It was just three weeks to Christmas Day.

Mary was buried about half a mile to the west of Clooneen in Mount Irwin cemetery, near Knocknaskeagh. The cemetery lies in a little valley by an old ruined church south of the Tobercurry road. There were few flowers for Mary's grave that winter day.

Mary was about forty years old when she died, and she had mothered ten children. Her gentle influence on the family had been profound, and everything changed without her. Her epitaph could be written in the words of Katherine Tynan's poem, "To The Beloved".

> There's a road that winds by the foot of the mountains
>> Where I run in my dreams and you come to meet me,
> With your blue eyes and cheeks' old roses,
>> The old fond smile that was quick to greet me.
> They are not the same, the fields and the mountains.

> There is something lost, there is something lonely,
>> The birds are singing, the streams are calling,
> The sun's the same, the wind in the meadows,
>> But o'er your grave are the shadows falling,
>> The soul is missing, and all is lonely.

Mary's wake was almost a replica of old Jack's the year before, except this time the Finns were joined by the Hannons rather than the Kanes.

One evening Tom came home late from his drayman's deliveries and found the living-room full of people. The peat fire burned bright in the hearth, the air was clouded with tobacco smoke, and through the haze he saw his father seated by the fireside, his right fist clutching his drink, his left arm beating time to the chorus of a rebel song. His brothers were seated on the floor by the fireside. Tom greeted the company cheerfully, then left the room to swill off the grime of the day. There he met Kate, who had put the twins to bed and was now by herself awaiting his return. Tom saw a look in Kate's eyes that reminded him of his mother. He knew at once that Kate wanted no part in the noisy gathering, and that she did not want the boys there either. Tom gave his sister a reassuring hug, went out and got the harness back on Old Charlie. He then returned to the living-room and rounded up his brothers.

The boys huddled together on the draycart, their coats buttoned up for warmth, and Tom drove them up the dirt path and on to Ballymote road. He sang as he jerked the reins and promised to show them the glory of Ballymote by night. But they never reached there. They were halted on the road and sent back. The people of Ballymote were guarding themselves against the inroads of the fever epidemic and did not welcome strangers in their midst. So the party drove homeward, the boys still not sure what was happening or why Tom had dragged them from the warmth of the fireside that winter night.

By the time Tom and his brothers returned few of the visitors remained. Kate had banked up the fire and was sitting by its side next to her father. It was not long before the last guest left. Kate busily tidied up the debris of the gathering, then she and her younger brothers went to bed. Tom and his father were left alone.

Paddy and Tom had grown close together ever since that evening in Frenchpark when together they had faced an unknown assassin. Tom was now the eldest son, and as such shared his father's confidences. After the shock of Mary's death, they both chewed over an aspiration they had in common, the prospect of starting life afresh in another country, free from the oppression of their heritage.

"America," said Tom.

Paddy gazed thoughtfully into the glowing fire as though he could see the flame of an old desire still burning there, but he knew that was not to be.

"Too late, Tom," he replied. "Not with all the children to care for. England it will have to be."

Paddy saw the look of disappointment on Tom's face, and had the empathy to understand. He too felt the urge of the caged bird to soar afar, but he knew his own wings were clipped. It was all too late, too late to dream and too late to argue.

"We'll start afresh lad, I promise you. The Lord knows it will not be for the want of trying." Then, as an afterthought, as if to close the matter he added, "If things don't work out well for you in England, I promise I'll never stand in your way if you want to pack your bags and go off to America. I do promise that."

Christmas came and went, and then the New Year with its hopes and resolutions. Only Paddy and Tom knew which way the wind was blowing for 1877. As the days passed Paddy's plans began to take shape, and the chief draughtsman was Flannery of Ballaghaderreen.

"What you'll be after, Paddy," he advised, "is a nice little pub in Manchester or Liverpool. There you'll be your own master, and there'll be trade enough from all the thirsty Irishmen over there."

The idea appealed to Paddy and Tom, and they discussed it at great length as they drove the draycart into Roscommon. The more they discussed it the more feasible and attractive it became.

Flannery had contacts in the trade across the Irish Sea, and he promised to keep his ears open for the first whisper of any licensed premises becoming available. So the dream quickly became a reality in Paddy's mind. His main consideration at the time was the disposal of his farm.

He took his younger brothers, James and Dominic, into his confidence. They agreed upon a consideration whereby Dominic would take possession of the farm and James would take the area of bogland that Paddy had shared with their father, Jack Finn. All things being settled by a shake of the hand, Paddy lived from day to day for good news from Flannery.

At last the day arrived when Flannery announced that he knew of a tenancy becoming vacant in Manchester, which he believed would suit Paddy's requirements. The time had come to make Kate a party to the project, for her co-operation was essential to the success of the enterprise. Paddy had been reluctant to take his daughter into his confidence because he could foresee the upheaval and additional burden it would cause her at a time when she had so recently taken on the task of being housewife and mother to the young children. Her reaction was better than he had feared.

"If you think that is best for us, dada," she said, "I'll manage."

So Paddy, in good heart and with high expectations, set out for England to appraise and be appraised. For a man who had never stepped out of Connaught it was quite an experience. The port of Belfast, the sea crossing, the port of Liverpool and the city of Manchester crowded his brain with new sights and new experiences; the tall buildings, the crowded streets, the ships, the trains, the horse-drawn trams, the whole panorama of Victorian urbanity jostled in his mind as his new world took shape. He returned to Clooneen, not only inwardly delighted at the deal he had made, but with the outward assurance of a widely travelled man of uncharted business potential.

With all the business of procurement of the public house and disposal of the farm completed the time came for Paddy and his children to say farewell to their relatives and friends and to leave their home for the last time. None of them was to see Clooneen again.

The property of the farm has been passed down through Dominic's family. Dominic married Anne McDermot Roe, and they had nine children: seven sons and two daughters. The elder daughter, Mary Theresa, married Joseph Doohan and the farm was passed down to their son, Kevin Doohan. In line to succession of the farm are Kevin's sons, Joseph and Jeremiah.

The blackthorn tree stood by the Owenmore a century after Michael's death. It was finally uprooted by Joseph Doohan who still knew it as "Michael's Bush". And the hill behind the farm is still known as "Paddy's Hill".

Manchester

Paddy Finn bartered his farm in Clooneen for a beerhouse in Hulme, Manchester, and as beerhouses and the Hulme he knew belong to a past world it is worthwhile to give his new trade and its locality a cursory examination.

The English tavern first came under legal scrutiny during the reign of Edward VI, when alehouse keepers were required to hold a licence to exercise their trade. From then until the Beerhouse Act of 1830 licences were granted by the judiciary after taking "recognizance against unlawful games and for good rule".

The 1830 Act permitted the Excise to grant a licence without recognizance to any ratepayer of low rates qualification who could provide a certificate confirming the rateable value of the property and pay the licence fee of two guineas. The Act was superseded by the Beerhouse Act of 1869 which restored to the judiciary the granting and withholding of licences for the retail sale of beer, ale and porter.

The 1830 Act induced a proliferation of beerhouses. In 1831 there were eleven licensed premises in Hulme to cater for a population of 9,624. By 1871 there were at least 530 licensed premises catering for a population of 74,731. During the forty intervening years the ratio had altered from one beerhouse to 875 inhabitants to one beerhouse to 140 inhabitants.

The 1869 Act stemmed the proliferation, and the brewers' growing interest and investment in their retail outlets gave some assurance that the beerhouses they supplied would be well managed and orderly. An effort was made to give the beerhouse a new air of respectability. A pretentious piece of reporting in the *Hulme Advertiser* on Christmas Eve 1869 on the change of ownership of the Shakespeare Inn, Chapman Street, depicts the ultimate in the new approach.

"This comfortable and well-fitted hostelry has recently changed hands, the present proprietor, Mr Charles Hall, having had considerable experience, has, we are glad to say, been able to gather around him a large and select circle of friends. To those who are wont to indulge in the luxury of a quiet weed, combined with a sparkling glass of John Barleycorn, they will have their wishes fully satisfied, in addition to a rich intellectual treat."

This seems a long way from the "specimens of Irish greatness gathered round O'Connor's bar".

Publicans advertised entertainment to attract trade. The proprietor of the Eagle and Child begged to inform his friends and the public that he intended to open his commodious room for a "Free and Easy" every Monday at seven o'clock; the Alexander Hotel offered a Select Harmonic Meeting on Saturday and Monday at seven o'clock; the Walnut Inn was more succinct with "Ale and Porter. Concert Room. Broadwood Piano".

This was the world Paddy Finn entered when he took over the Rising Sun in Bedford Street. There were eighteen beerhouses in the street and, of more importance to the Finn family, St. Wilfrid's Catholic Church and School.

When the church was opened in 1849 it was known as St. Wilfrid in the Fields, and there were complaints that it was sited too far out of the city. At that time, City Road, the approach to the city from the south, was only a cinder path, and the parishioners crossed a field of wheat to get to the church. To the south and south-west there was open countryside. Within the next thirty years industrial Manchester covered the fields with narrow, gas-lit streets of terraced houses, corner shops, beerhouses and workplaces. Today St. Wilfrid's church stands isolated from its past. The squat tower above its slated roof looks down on new school buildings. On one of its brick walls there is still a nameplate marked Clopton Street, but the old street has now gone, and in its place there is a pedestrian footpath named Clopton Walk. The Hulme that Paddy knew has virtually disappeared.

Hulme occupies an area of about one square mile to the south of the city. It is bounded to the north by the River Medlock and to the west by the River Irwell. The road from Chester branched into three approach roads to the city and these passed through Hulme as Chester Road, City Road and Stretford Road. As Hulme became developed they were interlinked by the busy roads of Lower Moss

Lane, York Street and Great Jackson Street. Bedford Street ran parallel with City Road from Lower Moss Lane to Great Jackson Street, cutting through York Street between City Road and Stretford Road.

Paddy's Rising Sun was at the city end of Bedford Street, close to where it ended at Great Jackson Street. It was near enough to the Gaythorn gasworks at the end of City Road to come within range of its smell and pollution when the wind blew from the north-west, as it often did.

The Rising Sun came into being in 1861 when the Walker & Homfray brewery converted the dwellinghouses at 7 and 9 Bedford Street into a beerhouse. The licensee paid an annual rent to the brewery and managed the beerhouse on its behalf. He was dependent upon the brewery for his supplies, and the continuity of his tenancy was subject to his satisfactory management. The Rising Sun was eventually closed in 1917 under the provisions of the Compensation Act of 1904 which empowered the Justices to close down public houses on the grounds of unsuitability or non-requirement.

Paddy's tenancy was probationary in so far as he had to satisfy the brewery that he was able to maintain a competitive outlet for its products, but by and large he was his own master, the envy of his customers who, after a long day's work in mill or factory, found as they approached the polished, oak-panelled bar with its sparkling glasses and shining brass, a sanctuary as welcome and as comforting as that found by the pilgrim as he approaches the candlelit altar after a day's journey. For a short space of time the weary outside world was forgotten and the fellowship of men enjoyed, and who was to know that this was the house of the devil masquerading as the house of God.

Paddy and Tom enjoyed the excitement of their new venture. With unrestricted licensing hours their work kept them busy most of the day, and when evening brought more bar trade they were ready to be convivial with their customers and drink with them as they listened to the scraps of conversation that threw glimmers of light upon the new world they had chosen. They absorbed the Mancunian dialect which pronounced Hulme as Hoom, enabling its inhabitants to parody the words of the hymn when they announced that they came "from Hulme all blessings flow". There was many an Irishman in Hulme and from the other side of the bar Paddy and

Tom could enjoy as much merriment whilst pulling the pumps as they had known by their fireside at the farm in Clooneen. And here they were their own masters. Here there was no reproachful look as the children were hurried off to bed. This was their place of business, a world apart from the living quarters which came under the domain of Kate.

Paddy was very strict about the bar being out of bounds to the children. Kate was, of course, the exception. There was always much cleaning and polishing to be done in the morning, and the sooner the better. That was woman's work, and sixteen-year-old Kate was the woman. Apart from that, Paddy made only one other concession. He would occasionally ask Kate if the twins could be spared to join him at the bar. If she consented the twins were overjoyed. They knew they were being invited into forbidden premises to play their game.

Paddy would sit with a twin on each knee and wager a pint of ale with a customer that he could not tell which was Rose and which was Molly. That seemed straightforward enough, but the twins applied their own rules. They had their mutual likes and dislikes. They also had an inbred telepathy. If they liked the customer they would spontaneously call out that he was right, whether he was or not. If they disliked him they would ruefully announce he was wrong, whichever he chose. Their performance over they would give Paddy a kiss and skip off back to Kate's territory, highly pleased with themselves.

Kate's day began very early. She was first downstairs to inspect the premises and decide her priorities. There was clearing up and cleaning in the drinking rooms, the fire to light, breakfasts to prepare, beds to make and the twins to get ready for school before the daily chores really began. It was all hustle and bustle and Kate coped with it well and cheerfully.

It was Bernard's daily duty to shepherd the twins down Bedford Street to St. Wilfrid's school, so he had a vested interest in Kate's efforts to get them out of the house in good time.

"Hurry up and take your time," Kate would call out to them as they dawdled over breakfast. Then there would be a bustling and a scuffling, which Bernard eyed impatiently, as they gathered their coats and made last-minute preparations for the day ahead. Finally, Kate would shoo them out of the door with the parting exclamation, "If you fall down don't wait to pick yourself up."

The twins loved her exuberance. Since Mary's death Kate had become a mother to her sisters. When their school friends would preface their remarks with "My mother says", the twins would say, "My sister Kate says . . ."

For Bernard the change of school was a mixed blessing. He soon discovered that he had exchanged the fearsome Mr Carberry for a virulent Irishman named Corrigan. The new headmaster was a small, squarely built, bearded man. His posture in class was to caress his beard with his left hand and flourish a long, leather strap in his right hand. In moments of anger, which were not infrequent, he would bite at his beard and twitch the strap, a sure indication that he was about to pounce upon some unfortunate offender. Bernard quickly learned that the principal virtue of scholarship lay in the ability to avoid trouble. It was a relief to get out of Mr Corrigan's class unscathed and relax during the lesson given by some gentler teacher. The main blessing of St. Wilfrid's school was that it lay just down the street. There was no longer the trudge along the Ballymote road in the wind and the rain. But he missed old school friends, the comfort and companionship of Martin Millmow, and most of all his mother's greeting as he returned home to the farm below the hill. There was sadness as well as joy in the life of the transplanted eight-year-old schoolboy.

For Kate life was vastly different in Bedford Street, and her domestic duties were more arduous. She accepted the heavier burden willingly and cheerfully as she came under the spell of her father's euphoria. In her capacity of housekeeper she played an important part in the enterprise that Paddy deemed would provide the family with an affluence undreamed of in Clooneen. Today's drudgery was a small price to pay for tomorrow's prosperity.

Everything was so different. The oil lamps and the peat fire glowing in the large stone fireplace were now replaced by gaslight and the sulphurous coal flames in an iron grate. The cooking pot swinging from its crane had gone. Now there was a large iron pan for stews and an oven in the cast-iron fireplace for roasting and baking. There were more rooms to be cleaned apart from the public rooms and bar, for which neither Paddy nor Tom claimed full responsibility, although each was willing to do his share. Then there was the cellar, which was not only a store room for the bar but also Kate's larder and cold room with a large stone slab on which you could set a jelly or keep meat and other perishables fresh.

The entrance to the cellar was off a narrow passage separating the bar from the living quarters. It was here that Kate one day found the way blocked by a half-drunken customer as she went to get butter from the slab. She faced him fearlessly and ordered him off the premises. It may have been the look in the girl's eyes or the sight of the kitchen knife in her hand that influenced the man, but he lurched off in the direction of the bar without further ado.

With the approach of winter the Finn family had its first experience of Manchester fog. The November fog enveloped the city in a cold, damp blanket that smothered the daylight and muted the noise of the streets. As darkness fell it was not possible to see more than an arm's length ahead. It was just possible to shuffle along the pavement from the Rising Sun to the Derbyshire Arms, a few doors along Bedford Street, but to proceed further, past the adjacent pawnbroker's shop and across Clopton Street to St. Wilfrid's church, would be folly. It was easy to get lost in your own street as you groped your way from the diffused blur of gaslight at one lamp-post, through the thick wall of fog, until you reached the next, and stopped to wonder exactly where you were. As for the other side of the street, that might have been in a different world.

The fog was Paddy's enemy. He gasped for breath as he fell victim of bronchitis, a common complaint among the inhabitants of that smoke-laden city. He dreaded going out into the dirty soup of air, seasoned with the sulphurous fumes from the nearby Gaythorn gasworks.

By December the air had cleared and everybody looked forward to Christmas with its promise of snow. Paddy resolved it was going to be a good Christmas for his family. The decorations in the public rooms overspilled into the living quarters. There was plenty to eat and drink, and Paddy was lavish with his presents. Christmas and New Year came and went among a festive blur of intoxication at the Rising Sun. January and February brought the bitter cold, and an uneasy sense within the family that all was not going well. Paddy battled with his bronchitis and became unusually moody.

The Rising Sun venture was going awry. Paddy conducted his business on the false premise that whilst there was money coming in the till there was money to spend on ale to be drunk freely. A serious cash flow problem evolved and Paddy had increasing difficulty in paying for the brewery's deliveries. He learned his lesson too late. There was no short-term solution to the problem, and as his tenancy was probationary he could not seek extended credit from the brewery, which was both his sole supplier and his landlord. The end came abruptly. The brewery refused to renew his licence, and Paddy found himself jobless and homeless.

The Rising Sun had a new manager, Walter Leader. He and his wife Eliza moved in with their four children, and Paddy and his family moved out to 118 Bedford Street. They were practically destitute. When there are too many mouths to feed the family breaks up. Patrick, Edward and James enlisted as boy cadets in the armed services to ensure a roof over their heads, clothes on their backs and food in their mouths for the next three years. Bernard started playing truant from school to take up a newspaper round in Whalley Range about a mile to the south. In a full week he could earn as much as three shillings. The temptation to play truant became strong and frequent and Bernard succumbed as often as he dared. Tom at last got a job as labourer in a chemical works.

Christmas 1878 had little cheer for the Finn family and prospects for the coming year were bleak. Paddy struggled through the winter with his bronchitis. The cheerful camaraderie of the Rising Sun was over. The regulars still gathered round the bar telling their stories to their new host, Walter Leader. Few thought or cared what happened to Paddy Finn and his family just down the street.

Kate, as housekeeper, had a grim struggle trying to make ends meet. Every penny was needed to provide essential food, heating and lighting for the household. She looked back on the days when her mother had managed to rear a large family in comparative ease, and was glad that Mary had been spared the heartache of having to leave the farm and the meadows of Clooneen to skimp and scrape in the mean streets of Manchester. Her frustration at not being able to provide sufficient frayed her temper and there were outbursts of rage. A few fortunately ended in laughter.

There was the outburst over the twins' hair. They had lovely black curls, but the with love of the opposite they envied the straight, blonde hair of one of their school friends. One day they asked her how she kept her hair so fair and straight.

"I wash it in washing soda," she explained jokingly.

The twins lost no time in trying out the treatment. Kate caught them in the act, and with much shouting and scolding plunged them in a tub of hot water, gave them a good scrubbing and sat them down in front of the fire to dry their hair. They looked so dejected as their curls began to tighten as dark as ever that Kate burst out laughing. The twins soon joined in. They loved to hear their sister laugh.

Then there was the incident of Bernard's rabbit. Ever since they came to Manchester Bernard had pestered Kate for a pet, but she always told him she had enough to do without looking after pets while he was out at school or playing.

One spring morning, Bernard brought home a packing case and asked Kate whether, as it was the month of Our Lady, he could make a May altar for the Blessed Mother. Gladly she acquiesced. She gave him a large sheet for an altar cloth and let him have the plaster statuette of the Madonna from her bedroom. Bernard busied himself preparing the altar in his room, and Kate was impressed with her brother's thoughtful devotion amid the stress of the daily round. All went well until some days later Kate noticed an unpleasant smell emanating from the altar. She shifted the packing case, and through the wire mesh that Bernard had nailed to the open back she met the gaze of a startled pet rabbit. That was the end of Bernard's May devotions.

Tom's job was at the other side of Chester Road in the Cornbrook Road chemical works owned by a manufacturing chemist named John Dale and managed by his son Richard. It was there that Tom became friendly with a fellow Irish labourer, Laurence Dunn from Westmeath, who lived with his wife Mary, a Wicklow girl, at 32 Dover Street, off Cornbrook Road. Tom told them about how his family came over from County Sligo and the misfortune that had befallen them over the Rising Sun. They were very sympathetic and Mary, who was still in her twenties, wondered how such a young girl as Kate could cope with the housekeeping. She had little to spare with only herself and Laurence to keep. In the end they all agreed that a shared rent and shared fuel and lighting was a worthwhile economy, and within a few months the Finns had moved in with the Dunns.

If the move was convenient for Tom's job it was equally inconvenient for the children's schooling. They had to go along Cornbrook Road, across Chester Road and through a maze of streets until they reached City Road in the vicinity of Bedford Street. One street they passed down was Tatton Street, where they frequently met up with other children on their way to St. Wilfrid's school. Bernard soon made friends with the boys from the Tatton Street area and was admitted into the Tatton Street Gang, eventually becoming its leader. It must be emphasised that Victorian street gangs were not delinquents, but youngsters who banded together for street games and any social recreation that came their way. The gang was a club of limited membership, without clubroom, entrance fee or annual subscription. Its leader gave impetus to its activities.

Paddy Finn died of bronchitis at 32 Dover Street on 25th February 1881. There are conflicting reports of his age. Bernard believed his father was forty-six years old when he died. The cemetery records give his age as fifty and the death certificate advances it to sixty. There is little doubt that Tom did not know his father's age and there seems no reason to contradict Bernard's assessment. Paddy was buried in St. Joseph's Catholic cemetery at Moston, about three miles north of the city centre. His death certificate gave his occupation as "commercial traveller", probably a euphemism concocted by Tom to describe the odd jobs done by his father after vacating the Rising Sun. Bernard recalled that each shovel of earth that was tossed on his father's coffin seemed to fall as a weight on his own heart as he stood by the graveside that cold winter day. In ten days time Bernard would be twelve and ready to leave school and face the world.

From the little we know of Paddy Finn it is not possible to draw a clear picture of the inner man. His life reflected the times and social environment in which he lived. He was a victim of his inheritance, like so many generations of Connaught Finns before him, an alien to the rulers of his homeland, practising an alien religion. He tried to escape and he failed. But in his attempt he opened the door a little for his children and their children. A century has passed since he died and the world has changed. When the butterflies are dancing over the sunlit meadows, who are left to remember the caterpillars?

Kate told her twin sisters, "We would be much better off if Dada had not been so generous."

Tom remembered his promise of four years ago. "If things don't work out well for you in England, I promise I'll never stand in your way if you want to pack your bags and go off to America. I do promise that."

The four years in Manchester had moulded Bernard's outlook into a pattern that was to last his lifetime. His convictions became set. He would escape the poverty and deprivation, and he would not fail because of drink or other moral frailty.

From almost infancy he pledged himself to total abstinence. He neither drank anything alcoholic nor smoked tobacco throughout his life. Whilst the family was still at the Rising Sun he joined the temperance movement.

The movement was strongly rooted in Manchester at that time. The Rechabites, founded in 1835, had run a branch in Great Jackson Street since 1843. The Band of Hope, founded in 1847 as a temperance organisation for children, had branches in Hulme as did the Church of England Total Abstinence Society, founded in 1862.

Bernard chose a group called the Crusaders run by a second-hand furniture dealer named McClernon, a Toby Weller figure of a man who was assisted by a thin sliver of a man named O'Neill. Each had a stock speech which they delivered every Sunday evening at the regular meetings of the group.

Bernard soon knew the speeches by heart, and from time to time he would mount a soap-box, at the behest of the Tatton Street gang, and entertain them with his version of the McClernon speech, a vivid caricature in words and gesture of the Scottish orator.

Some Sundays he would persuade members of the gang to attend the Crusaders' meeting and see and hear the original for themselves. On one such occasion McClernon was too sick to take the chair and O'Neill had to conduct the meeting alone. With some apprehension he embarked on his stock speech.

"When I first came to Manchester," he began, "I was a drinking man. I arrived at Victoria Station without a penny in my pocket. That was how low I had sunk. I resolved there and then to take the pledge and give up drink for ever. Now I can put my hand in my pocket and instead of searching for the odd penny, I can find plenty of shillings there." Here he plunged his hand into his trouser pocket and rattled its contents vigorously in confirmation of his words. "I advise you one and all," he concluded, "all you who have not taken the pledge, do not waste any more time, but join the Crusaders now."

His brief flash of introductory oratory ended, he was uncertain how to proceed in the absence of the principal speaker. He jingled his money again, took a sip of water and then told his audience how distressed he was at the enforced absence of the chief Crusader.

"If any of you," he ventured hesitatingly, "would care to oblige with a few remarks on the virtues of temperance, now is the time."

There was an unresponsive silence, broken only by the uneasy shuffling of feet. Then a few vague mutterings from the back of the room exploded into the rallying cry of "Finn! Finn!"

O'Neill beamed with pleasure and relief as he watched two of the Tatton Street gang propel Bernard towards the platform, followed by about half a dozen others to ensure he got there.

From the platform Bernard looked down with some trepidation at the mass of faces below him, the grins of the street urchins and the serious countenances of the older people. To gain time and composure he poured himself a glass of water from the bottle on the table and took a sip amid cheers from the Tatton Street clique on the back seats. He tugged at his waistcoat to more cheering and, his confidence somewhat restored, he gave a preliminary cough to clear his throat and launched himself into the McClernon stock speech.

Each time he waved his arms to denounce the "beggarly elements of intoxicating dr-r-rink", he brought the house down. It was a precocious but spirited performance. The wild delight of his young adherents infected the whole assembly. Never again in his lifetime was his oratory to receive so tumultuous a reception.

The priest who attended Paddy on his deathbed helped Bernard to get his first job as bobbin boy in a Manchester silk mill. His wages were four shillings a week compared with the irregular three shillings a week he was earning from his paper round during his frequent spells of truancy. He was just twelve years old when he began full-time employment.

At the silk mill he encountered for the first time the ribaldry of the factory floor. He was much teased by the mill girls, who made mock sexual advances towards him as he changed their bobbins. But behind the vulgarity there was the innate friendliness of the Lancashire workpeople. Bernard remembered with gratitude the kindness of one of the weavers, a Mrs Kate Austen, who took pity on "the poor, half-starved Irish bugger" and took him home with her one evening to share the family supper.

Paddy Finn died shortly before the census of 1881 was taken. The census records the residents of 32 Dover Street on 8th April 1881 as being Tom Finn, aged twenty-one, chemical labourer; Kate Finn, aged nineteen, housekeeper; Bernard Finn, aged fourteen, silk weaver; Roseanne and Maria Finn, aged nine, scholars — all from Sligo, Ireland — together with Laurence Dunn, labourer, aged thirty-three, and Mary Dunn, aged thirty, from Westmeath and

Wicklow, Ireland, respectively. The omission of Patrick, Edward and James Finn from the records confirms they had all left home by that time.

The ages recorded for Bernard and the twins conflict with their birth records which indicate that Bernard had just passed his twelfth birthday and that the twins were still eight years old. There is little doubt that Bernard was confused about his age whilst in Manchester as he believed he was thirteen when his father died and that he was five years older than the twins. Such confusion was very common in those days and raises some doubt about the recorded ages of Tom and Kate, both of whom were born before official birth records were kept. What appears evident, however, is that Tom was older than Kate and that there is no real reason to suppose that their ages differed from those declared in the census.

Edward, Paddy's sixth son, was the first of the Finn children named in the official record of births. He was born on 14th May 1865 and was approaching his sixteenth birthday when the census was taken. He was the youngest of the trio of boy soldiers who left home after the collapse of Paddy's business at the Rising Sun.

There was always great excitement in Dover Street when any of the trio returned home on leave in their colourful uniforms and pill-box hats. The twins had heard that the soldier maintained his erect military bearing by wearing corsets, and giggled with delight at the thought of their brothers being clothed in such attire.

After the three-year cadet service, James opted to return to civilian life, but Patrick and Edward were recruited into the regular forces. Edward was stationed at Portland harbour, near Weymouth. He joined the Royal Marines. Patrick made his career in the regular army and was eventually drafted for active service in Egypt and the Sudan.

Bernard gave up his job at the silk mill within a few months for more remunerative employment at the warehouse of Ralli Brothers in Peter Street, opposite the Free Trade Hall. The firm baled and warehoused cotton goods, mainly for export to India and Ceylon. Bernard operated a small machine in the warehouse basement that cut and riveted the metal baling hoops. His new job not only paid more than the silk mill, but offered additional remuneration through overtime work.

The site of the warehouse was at one time in St. Peter's Field, an area of open land which took its name from St. Peter's church close by. It was here that people from the nearby Lancashire mill towns assembled in 1819 to demonstrate for fuller representation in the House of Commons.

The local magistrates had been invited to attend the assembly, but on learning its likely size they feared a breach of the peace. Over a thousand troops were posted around the area in strategic positions in case of disturbance, and a double rank of special constables armed with batons were detailed to line the route to the speakers' platform.

On the morning of the 16th August 1819, the crowds marched into St. Peter's Field in good order with bands playing and banners flying. Girls dressed in white danced and sang as they went. Shortly after midday sixty thousand people, including women and children, had assembled. They sang the National Anthem as they awaited the arrival of the speakers. Meanwhile the panic-stricken magistrates had spent the morning at a house in the vicinity undecided what to do. Finally they handed the Deputy Chief Constable a warrant for the arrest of Mr Henry Hunt, the principal speaker, should he address the gathering.

The Deputy Chief Constable's response was far from assuring. He told the magistrates that he had insufficient constables to control the disturbance he expected would arise from the execution of the warrant. Thereupon the magistrates agreed to provide military assistance if necessary.

Mr Hunt arrived on the platform at one o'clock and began his address. He was arrested and the troops were called to disperse the crowd. At first the action was indecisive as raw recruits jostled almost good-humouredly among the assembly. Then the 15th Hussars were ordered to advance with drawn sabres. They cleared the field in ten minutes. Eleven people were killed and almost six hundred injured in the charge which became known as "Peterloo", in ironic memory of Wellington's victory over Napoleon Bonaparte at Waterloo four years earlier. Henry Hunt was sentenced to thirty months imprisonment for presiding at an unlawful meeting.

The Manchester that Bernard grew to know when he worked in the city warehouse had vastly changed since those days, as it grew in substance and importance with the industrialisation of spinning and weaving. A new and much larger Stock Exchange was completed in 1874. The new Town Hall building in Albert Square, acclaimed to be the finest in Europe, was opened in 1877. The old

Town Hall, opened in 1825, stood on the site of the house of Dr Charles White, a founder of Manchester Infirmary, at the corner of Cross Street and King Street. With the opening of the new Town Hall the building was converted into Manchester Reference Library. When Bernard began work the new Central Station, with its great span of glass roofing, had just been completed as a terminus for the Great Northern, the Midland and the Cheshire Lines railways. Tracks were still being laid in the streets to extend the horse-drawn tramway system.

Bernard had grown accustomed to factory-floor ribaldry during his few months at the silk mill, but there it was mainly good-natured teasing from the mill girls. At the warehouse he experienced the vindictiveness shown to Catholics generally in those days and to Irish Catholics in particular. It was his misfortune that his persecutors were supplied with ready ammunition from a series of lectures given in Manchester by Edith O'Gorman, who described herself as an escaped nun. They hurled at him gross obscenities abstracted from her lectures, and made his life a misery. He felt totally inadequate to counter their jibes until one day, as he was leaving for home, a young colleague named Waterhouse passed him a slip of paper on which was scribbled a list of book titles and the message, "See these in the public library".

The message transformed Bernard's approach to life. He was an intelligent child whose meagre education had been truncated by truancy on the Whalley Range newspaper round. He quickly became an avid and thoughtful reader. The library was in easy reach and each Saturday, as soon as the warehouse had closed, he would pick up a book for reading over the weekend.

At first his reading was mainly confined to the novels of Charles Dickens, but later he became acquainted with the works of Henry George, the American political economist, and of Herbert Spencer, whose *Principles of Psychology* fascinated him by the overpowering quality of its vocabulary. He was particularly impressed by Spencer's definition of evolution. By a long and painful process he succeeded in committing it to memory to hold it in readiness for the next time he was assailed at the warehouse for his beliefs.

One lunchtime he steered the inevitable argument to the subject of evolution of religion before and after the Reformation.

"Before we begin," cautioned Bernard, "we should have a

definition of terms. I bet none of you knows what is meant by evolution, let alone religion."

His tormentors exchanged glances, but remained silent. Waterhouse smiled encouragingly and invited him to go ahead. With an intent gaze at the ceiling to refresh his memory Bernard recited Spencer's definition.

"Evolution is an integration of matter and a concomitant dissipation of motion, during which the motion passes from an indefinite, incoherent homogeneity to a definite, coherent heterogeneity and during which the retained motion undergoes a parallel transformation."

He paused, hoping no one would ask him to spell or define any polysyllabic term. His fears were groundless. His tormentors had shuffled away to other pursuits. The young defender of the faith had evolved into a precocious young prig. Only Waterhouse remained to congratulate him.

Shortly afterwards, Bernard noticed in the *Umpire*, a Manchester Sunday newspaper of the time, an article on the evolution of progress in sport and politics and similar human endeavour. It was written by a columnist under the pseudonym "Nunquam", who argued that in accordance with the law of evolution the fittest survived and the unfit perished. As a recognised authority on the subject Bernard wrote him a letter disagreeing with some of his conclusions. To his surprise and delight his words appeared in the *Umpire* with the author's identity concealed under the name "Bernardus". Bernard was glad and grateful that his identity had been kept secret, but he was proud to see his words in print.

All was not misery at the warehouse. Bernard had charm and a good sense of humour. His cheerful, freckled face earned him many friends, among whom was Tom Sumner. Early in 1882 Tom organised a warehouse sweepstake on the forthcoming Liverpool steeplechase, the Grand National, in which the participants drew a blank or a horse according to their luck. Most were blanks.

Bernard had no interest in horse-racing or betting, and the sweep was practically complete before Tom approached him and asked if he would like to try his luck. Bernard had a spare shilling or two at the time, and as the race would be the talk of the warehouse in the weeks to come he did not want to be left out. Much to Tom's surprise he agreed to enter the sweep.

"All the horses except one have already been drawn," Tom

warned. "All the rest are blanks. I reckon your chances of picking the winner are no more than sixty-six to one."

Undeterred, Bernard handed Tom the stake money and drew a slip of paper from the few remaining. He was lucky. He chose the last runner left in the sweep, a horse called Seaman. He made no mention of his good fortune at home, being ashamed to admit that he had squandered his hard-earned money.

As the day of the race drew nearer Bernard was offered various premiums above his stake money for the sale of his ticket to those who had drawn blanks, but he was caught up in the excitement of the occasion and refused all offers. Indeed, when Tom Sumner hired a wagonette to take the enthusiasts to watch the race Bernard was the first to book a seat.

The party drove off from Peter Street in fine style. The punters swayed on their facing benches as the driver, with a large rosette in his top hat, flicked his whip at the horses. The wagonette rattled down Deansgate, crossed the River Irwell in Salford, and headed for the East Lancashire Road to take them on their thirty-five-mile journey to Liverpool and the Aintree racecourse.

The crowds were thronging the course when the wagonette reached Aintree. The bookmakers were busy taking bets and feverishly ticktacking changes in starting prices. Only twelve runners came under starter's orders that year, the favourite being Cloister. Bernard's horse, Seaman, was being ridden by its owner, Lord Manners. There was much excitement in Tom Sumner's party as the runners trotted to the starting line. Then they were off.

Bernard saw little of the race. The horses disappeared in the distance and there was much speculation among the crowd as to which horse had fallen at what particular jump. Bernard listened intently to each rumour to hear whether Seaman's name had been mentioned. Then a cheer went up as the leaders cleared the last fence and the colours of Cloister, the favourite, were seen among them. The favourite raced to the finishing post, but another horse beat him to it. It was Seaman. Seaman won the Grand National, and Bernard won £20.

As he clambered back into the wagonette he felt he was one of the richest boys in the world. The homeward journey was a cheerful epilogue to the race meeting. The wagonette stopped at almost every public house along the East Lancashire Road. Only Bernard and the horses drank water. When the driver at last found his way back to Peter Street there was much back slapping as the exuberant punters lurched off the wagonette singing "For he's a jolly good fellow".

On his way back to Dover Street Bernard pondered on how best to make use of his newly won fortune. It did not take him long to decide. With it he would buy Kate what she had yearned for since she came to Manchester, a sewing machine. And there might be money in hand to buy material to sew dresses for herself and the twins. Bernard was no believer in easy come, easy go. He wanted to invest his windfall to the greatest benefit of his sisters, and that he did, to Kate's deep-felt gratitude.

There followed a series of happenings in the Finn family, entirely separate in themselves, but in an obscure way interrelated. James forsook a military career after his three years' compulsory service and returned home. Tom let his job at the Cornbrook Road chemical works and emigrated to the United States. And Kate fell in love.

James returned to civilian life at a time of a strained relationship between the United Kingdom and Egypt. British interests in Egypt stemmed from its purchase of shares in the Egyptian company Canal Maritime de Suez to prevent the possibility of a French monopoly in the running of the Suez Canal. Trouble broke out early in 1882 after the appointment of Arabi Pasha as Egyptian War Minister. Resentment of British and French interests in Egypt led to rioting in the streets of Alexandria, and there was deep concern for the safety of British and French nationals throughout Egypt. On 11th July the British fleet bombarded Alexandria, and by September a British expeditionary force under the command of Sir Garnet Wolseley entered Egypt and occupied Cairo. Arabi Pasha was made prisoner and was banished from Egypt. But there was greater trouble the following year when the fanatical followers of Mohammed Ahmed, the Madhi, overran the Sudan and destroyed an Egyptian army under the command of Hicks Pasha. In January 1884 the British Government sent General Gordon to Khartoum to organise a planned evacuation of the Sudan, but when the insurrectionists besieged Khartoum, Gordon refused to leave his post. Lord Wolseley led an expedition into the Sudan to lift the siege and rescue Gordon, but its progress down the Nile was slow and halting. On 26th January 1885 Khartoum fell, and Gordon was assassinated as he descended the outer staircase of the palace to parley with the invaders.

Patrick, who chose to remain in the regular army, was drafted for active service in Egypt and the Sudan and, like many a young soldier, he embarked with thoughts of the girl he had left behind. He had fallen in love with a pretty, dark-haired Irish girl named Lucy Doyle, the daughter of a Dublin barrister, but was too shy to propose to her. Whilst he was on active service he bitterly regretted his timidity, for he discovered she had married another soldier named William Owen.

As for Brother Edward, he opted for the Royal Marines and was thereby destined for a life far removed from his brothers and sisters.

James returned to a household struggling in a morass of poverty, and at a time when Tom, the head of the household, and Kate, the housekeeper, were at loggerheads over Tom's proposals to escape from their environment.

"We can all go to America," pleaded Tom. "I'll go first and get a job, and in a month or two I'll be able to send you the passage money for you all to join me, and we can start a new life over there just as Dada wanted."

"More likely leave us here to starve," retorted Kate. "Dada had grand ideas when we came to England. Fine words don't butter any parsnips, Tom. You just have no idea what it takes to bring up a family. Mama knew, but neither you nor Dada knew when you mapped out our future in Clooneen after she was gone. We need you here, Tom, not in America."

James quickly realised that his presence acted as a casting vote in the argument as far as Tom was concerned. With two wage earners in the household he could pursue his emigration plans with a clear conscience no matter what Kate said. She would soon find that he was right when they were all safely in America.

So James's homecoming was the signal for Tom's emigration, and Tom's emigration was the signal for Frank Glover to enter Kate's life in earnest.

Frank Glover was an asthmatic young cook, the son of William Glover, a painter and decorator. Whether he was a Mancunian is doubtful. It seems more likely that the Glovers came from some other part of Lancashire, and that Frank had come to Manchester to work. It seems that he left very little impression on the Finn family, perhaps because they regarded him as an intruder bent on depriving them of their sister and little mother.

Tom's departure and Frank Glover's entrance precipitated the

Finns' vacation of the house in Dover Street, which had the sole merit of being near Tom's place of work. In 1884 they moved to 86 Duke Street in the vicinity of St. Wilfrid's school and church, and Frank Glover took up residence with them. That summer Kate became pregnant, and she and Frank Glover were married at St. Wilfrid's church on 15th December. Kate was then twenty-three years old and Frank Glover was twenty-six. The marriage was witnessed by Kate's brother James and by Eliza Ann Isherwood.

The identity of Eliza Ann Isherwood has been lost in the mists of time. She may have been the daughter of Fanny Eliza Isherwood, who kept the Derbyshire Arms at 25 Bedford Street at the time when Paddy kept the Rising Sun, and so could have been Kate's first friend in Manchester. But this is sheer speculation. Fanny Isherwood vacated her tenancy shortly after Paddy and went to live at 110 Cornbrook Street. No trace of her has been retained in family folklore, and Kate's husband, Frank Glover, remains a shadowy figure.

There are only fragmented memories passed down by the twins of life at 86 Duke Street, and of their childhood in Manchester. Molly recalled Duke Street as being quite a nice street in those days. She remembered the occasion when Bernard hanged her doll, using a gas bracket as the gallows. Roseanne remembered James waking her and Molly one morning and telling them to get up quickly as there was a man in the house. He raced downstairs, and as the girls appeared at the top of the staircase he grinned up at them, made a polite bow and called out, "Behold a man." It was Jimmy Finn's twenty-first birthday.

In May 1885 Kate and Frank Glover's baby was born, a son they called Edward. Shortly after Edward's birth, the Glovers and Finns left Duke Street and resettled in 25 Pownall Street, just off Duke Street.

It was about that time that Bernard enlisted in the Volunteer Force which some years later, in 1908, combined with the Imperial Yeomanry to form the Territorial Force, renamed the Territorial Army in 1921.

Bernard was under age when he enlisted, but his height and build satisfied the recruiting sergeant's requirements without any awkward questions being asked. He was recruited into the 17th Lancashire Regiment, popularly known as the Salford Volunteers through the location of its headquarters in Cross Lane, Salford.

For Bernard the chief attraction, and possibly the sole purpose of enrolment, was the annual fortnight under canvas at Kinmel Bay, near the North Wales seaside resort of Rhyl. The training in camp included a route march nineteen miles down the Vale of Clwyd to the town of Rhuddlan and its moated castle, built as the head-quarters of Edward the First in his campaign to conquer Wales and site of the Treaty of Rhuddlan which confirmed his sovereignty in 1284.

Now, six centuries later, Bernard and his fellow Volunteers marched into Rhuddlan with shoulders braced and arms swinging, for there were pretty Welsh girls out in the streets awaiting their arrival. The march ended at the ruined castle and the Volunteers were served lunch in its grounds. The band played dance music in the great hall. There was time to relax and enjoy oneself before being called back into rank to start the nineteen miles return march to Rhyl.

The days spent in Wales were a welcome relief to Bernard after twelve months work at the warehouse. They enabled him to journey up the Conwy Valley and see the Snowdon range of mountains beyond Capel Curig, as well as to taste the pleasures of the coastal resorts. The peace and tranquillity of Snowdonia must have reminded him of the days of his early childhood when the world about him was small and unspoilt.

Bernard was a Volunteer for two years only. After that he had to finance his own holidays. He took two holidays in the Isle of Man with Tom Sumner and two older colleagues from the warehouse. On the first crossing his companions advised him how to avoid seasickness, but their advice was not heeded, because he proved to be a good sailor, which was more than can be said for his advisers, all of whom were seasick. Leaving them to their misery, Bernard sauntered round the deck and noticed a vaguely familiar figure propped up against the mainmast. The eyes were closed and he could hear an occasional moan coming from the blue, bearded lips. It was Mr Corrigan, his former headmaster at St. Wilfrid's school. Bernard lost no time in rousing his ailing comrades to come and join him as he gloated over the misfortunes of the stricken tyrant.

In 1886 there came to Manchester a man whom Bernard regarded as a demi-god, William Ewart Gladstone, the Prime Minister. The scholarship and tolerance of Gladstone had made a lasting impression on Bernard ever since he read a verbatim report in

The Nineteenth Century of a theological debate between the Grand Old Man and Cardinals Manning and Newman. It was too profound to digest thoroughly, but he absorbed enough to jar an innate conviction that everything uttered by his clerical and lay tutors was unequivocally right and true.

Mr Gladstone was speaking in Manchester Free Trade Hall in Peter Street on Home Rule for Ireland, but despite a most enthusiastic reception his oratory was of little avail. Ireland was his downfall when he called a General Election the following year. The Liberals were defeated and a Conservative Government was elected under the leadership of Lord Salisbury.

In 1887 Manchester celebrated the Golden Jubilee marking the fiftieth year of the reign of Queen Victoria. Prince Albert, the Prince Consort, came to Manchester to open the great Jubilee Exhibition held in the Horticultural Gardens at Old Trafford.

But amid all the festivities the greatest attraction for Bernard was the visit of two Americans. Colonel William Cody, the legendary "Buffalo Bill" of schoolboy fiction, brought over his Wild West show. The other American hero was John L. Sullivan, who appeared in Manchester as "The Fistic Marvel" and offered prize-money to any spectator who could last five rounds in the ring with him.

The Golden Jubilee year ended badly for Bernard. The warehouse manager at Ralli Brothers, Charles Politachi, had always practised stringent economy, usually involving longer working hours for less pay. He now embarked upon the elimination of what he considered to be unnecessary labour. He decided that Bernard's work could be done by the packers themselves and promptly dismissed Bernard with no more compassion than if he were discarding an obsolete piece of machinery.

At the time of his dismissal Bernard was earning between £1 2s 6d and £1 5s 0d (£1.25) a week depending on the amount of overtime worked, and his wages provided a substantial contribution to the household income.

The years spent in the warehouse cellar had done nothing to enhance his physical well-being. He had started work as a freckled, round-faced boy, able to hold his own with the English warehouse boys who were always ready to pick a fight with the alien Irish. He finished his employment a tall, thin youth, pale and anaemic, weighing only ten stones.

Bernard hated to be a financial burden to his family and desperately sought work without successs. He had begun to regard his prospects as hopeless when an employment agency put him in touch with a man named Blades who managed the Palace Hotel at Buxton. There was a vacancy for the job of hotel porter at a wage of fourteen shillings a week, free board and lodging and uniform provided. Bernard was selected from a number of applicants, and so left Manchester to begin a new episode of his life.

Buxton is a pleasant Derbyshire spa situated twenty-five miles south-east of Manchester. Its medicinal spring gushing from below the limestone escarpment was used by the Romans who built a bath to hold its waters. In the Middle Ages a shrine was built by the spring and named St. Anne's Well and listed as one of the holy wells of England. After the Reformation the shrine was closed, but its waters continued to attract the sick.

In Elizabethan times the spa was visited by many of the nobility, and in 1570 the Earl of Shrewsbury, custodian of the captive Mary, Queen of Scots, built the hall to accomodate the most distinguished visitors to the town.

The land and neighbouring estates were largely held by the Cavendish family. Sir William Cavendish was Gentleman-Usher to Cardinal Wolsley and was granted monastic lands upon the dissolution of the monasteries. After his death in 1577 his widow married George, Earl of Shrewsbury. His descendants became the Dukes of Devonshire.

William Cavendish, 1st Duke of Devonshire, was born in 1640. The family seat at Chatsworth was not completed until the year of his death, 1707. The Dukes of Devonshire maintained not only Chatsworth and the neighbouring Hardwick Hall, built by the Elizabethan widow who become Countess of Shrewsbury, but also Bolton Abbey, Lismore Castle, Compton Place and London residences at Devonshire House and Burlington House.

In 1781 the 5th Duke used the accumulated profits of his copper mines to construct an elegantly designed Crescent near to the Buxton spring. The Roman bath was filled in and buried within the foundations of the Crescent. The Duke was also responsible for the construction of the Great Stables on the rising ground to the east of the Crescent. The complex was designed to provide accommodation for the coachmen and grooms, shelter for the carriages and stabling for up to three hundred horses. In 1858 the 6th Duke made a charitable bequest of the property for use as the Devonshire Royal Hospital. The central courtyard was roofed by a superb dome in 1879, at that time recognised as the largest dome in the world.

The Palace Hotel where Bernard came to work was commissioned by the 7th Duke and designed by his architect, Henry Currey. It was built on the hill behind the Devonshire Hospital, close to the railway station.

At the time of Bernard's arrival the Duke was developing the spa with the construction of the Pavilion, an ornate circular building made largely of glass framed in cast iron, which was to house a concert hall, theatre and ballroom. Its conservatories overlooked the Pavilion Gardens that extend along the banks of the River Wye.

Bernard's duties as hotel porter included meeting visitors at the nearby railway station and conveying their luggage to the hotel. From the outset he disliked the work, mainly because of the servility engendered from the practice of tipping. As gratuities formed part of his remuneration he soon became out of pocket, especially as he refused on principle to join the line of servants expectantly awaiting the departure of each guest. The only satisfaction he seems to have derived from the work was in observing a new stratum of society and a way of living that he had not experienced before.

Buxton still attracted peers of the realm and some stayed at the Palace Hotel. One whom Bernard remembered well was Lord Egerton, a pleasant old gentleman who, when the weather turned chill, would take off his shoes and sit in front of the fire in the hall of the hotel warming his stockinged feet. His geniality and informality, however, did not extend beyond the boundary of propriety he rigidly kept between peer and commoner and master and servant.

Bernard's Lord Egerton was most likely Baron Egerton of Tatton, who was born in 1832 and would be in his late fifties when Bernard met him. He was at that time chairman of the Manchester Ship Canal Company and had been responsible for raising the £8 million capital required to proceed with the construction of the canal that in the next decade was to make Manchester a port by carrying sea-going vessls from the Mersey estuary to the Old Trafford dockland.

The Tatton family seat was set in a thousand-acre park near Knutsford. His estates included the nearby village of Rostherne, where he had recently restored the old parish church of St. Mary to mark the 700th year of its foundation. Beside the church is Rostherne Mere, one of the largest and deepest meres in Cheshire. It is about a hundred acres in area and has a depth of a hundred feet. Local tradition regarded it as fathomless, and there is a legend that when the bells were first being hung in St. Mary's church tower the largest of them fell and rolled down into the mere. Each Easter morning, it was said, a mermaid would raise it from the water and as she did so the bell would toll.

During his stay at Buxton, Bernard kept in touch with his brother Tom who was working on the railroad at Fort Scott, Kansas. Basically unhappy with his lot at the hotel, he was always interested in news from America. He also got in touch with a girl cousin of about his own age who was living in Cincinnati who urged him to migrate to "this land of free men". Only two Americans visited the Palace Hotel whilst he was employed there. Both came from St. Louis. One was in the tobacco and cigar business, his companion managed a hotel.

On 22nd June 1889, Frank Glover died of asthma. Kate was left a widow at twenty-eight with a son of four. Alive, Frank Glover seems to have made little impression among his Finn in-laws, but his death was followed by a stir in the family similar to that following the death of Paddy eight years before.

After the death of Frank Glover, Bernard appeared in the Manchester Street Directory as occupier of 25 Pownall Street (occupation silk weaver). His nomination indicates that James had left the family home for the last time. There remained resident in Pownall Street Kate and her young son and her twin sisters.

The sewing machine that Bernard had bought his sisters had been put to good use. Kate was an accomplished dressmaker and the twins were employed as seamstresses at Affleck & Brown, one of Manchester's largest fashion stores.

The fact that his sisters were self-supporting, and indirectly through his agency, probably swayed Bernard into making the greatest decision in his young life, to leave the job he hated and join Tom in America. He had a stand-up row with the hotel manager and his wife, chiefly with Mrs Blades, and was once again unemployed. But this time he knew exactly where his destiny lay. He wrote to Tom and his Cincinnati cousin and prepared for his emigration. During his stay at Buxton he had amassed savings of £20. A steerage passage to New York cost £4 and he reckoned he would have sufficient money in hand to join Tom and start a new life.

As he made the rail journey back to Manchester he smiled wryly as he remembered that his savings from nearly two years of drudgery were equal to his winnings on that heady afternoon at Aintree over seven years ago. Then he was a young boy, now he was a man ready to face all that life had in store. But one thing remained the same. He dared not tell Kate. Too well he remembered the bitter confrontation when Tom broke the news of his impending emigration. Was it possible that the seventeen-year-old twins could keep a secret without raising Kate's suspicions or without inadvertently making an indiscreet remark in young Edward's hearing that might be transmitted to Kate? He decided to keep his plans to himself until his passage had been confirmed.

All went well. The twins were told, and so great was the excitement that Bernard deemed it politic to tell Kate that he was going to see their relatives in Ireland. As far as his true destination was concerned Roseanne and Molly were sworn to absolute secrecy. How they managed to keep the secret they never knew, especially as the great day came imminent.

Kate joined in the enthusiasm, and when the morning of departure arrived she made sandwiches for Bernard to take on the journey. He packed them in a Gladstone bag with his clothing and crockery and cutlery for the voyage, as steerage passengers had to provide their own tableware. Last in the bag was a bottle of brandy slipped in by James.

"Good for seasickness," he said. "If you feel yourself getting giddy, take a snort. If you become seasick anyway, take a snifter."

Bernard embarked for New York on the Cunard liner *Servia* on 28th February 1890. Early in the voyage he felt queasy and decided to have a snort of James' brandy. The snort induced vomiting. He did not risk a snifter.

The feeding arrangements for the steerage passengers reminded Bernard of the way his mother used to feed their hens from the leftovers of the Clooneen dinner table. He was so repulsed that he permitted himself the extravagance of investing another £1 of his remaining savings for the privilege of eating with the stewards at their table. The investment was well worth while. He was able to eat three good meals a day without feeling seasick. He gave the brandy to two young Americans he found shivering on the steerage deck.

They were so grateful that they promised him a warm welcome in their home town of Danville, Virginia, if ever he passed that way.

The *Servia* docked in New York harbour on 9th March 1890, two days after Bernard's twenty-first birthday.

That spring Kate became pregnant again. There may be substance in the story that her new lover was killed in an accident before her baby was born, but there is no record of his identity or fate. Her second son, Vincent Glover, was born in February 1881.

Shortly afterwards the three Finn sisters left Pownall Street to go their different ways. Kate and Roseanne found homes for themselves in Charlton-on-Medlock and Molly went to Aldershot to live with their brother Patrick.

Patrick's soldiering in Egypt and the Sudan ended with his being invalided home with amoebic dysentry with the rank of sergeant. He got a transfer to the Medical Corps and was posted to the Cambridge Military Hospital, Aldershot. By good fortune he met his first love, Lucy Doyle, again. Her husband, William Owen, was dead and she was a widow with three children, two sons named William and Andrew, and a daughter named Frances. Patrick was determined not to lose Lucy again. They married and settled down to life among the military community of Aldershot. Their first baby, a son named Ernest, was born in 1889. Their second baby, a daughter named Florence, was born in 1893. Shortly after her birth Ernest died.

It is difficult to determine how many years had passed since Molly had last seen her brother Patrick. A studio photograph of Patrick, Bernard and the twins testifies that Patrick had returned to Manchester on at least one occasion after the death of his father.

In the photograph Patrick is seated between the twins. He is wearing a single-breasted suit with high, narrow lapels. His waistcoat is cut high with a fobchain suspended from one of its many buttonholes. Above the waistcoat is a high, white collar and white tie. He has a young face, quiffed hair and drooping moustache.

The twins have faces of young girls, but their dress is adult. Although not dressed identically, each is wearing a wide-lapelled bodice buttoned down to an hour-glass waistline. From the gorgets around their throats a cravat billows into the front of the bodice. Each has a toecap peeping out from under a voluminous pleated skirt.

Bernard stands behind the trio, a tall figure in a close-fitting,

Roseanne, Patrick, Bernard and Maria Finn. Our earliest picture of the
Finn family, taken in about 1890. Preserved all these years by
Florence Finn Hughes.

single-breasted jacket buttoned up to high, narrow lapels which almost conceal a strip of white collar and the knot of his tie.

The studio backcloth in the photograph depicts the corner of an altar and what appears to be an ornate window.

In trying to assess when and upon what occasion the photograph was taken it is important to judge the ages of the quartet at the time. Paddy's fourth son, Patrick, could have been born in either 1860 or 1862, making him one year older or one year younger than Kate.

If we take Kate's wedding in December 1884 as the first likely occasion upon which the photograph could have been taken, Patrick would be twenty-two or twenty-four at the time. That would have given him time to have been in the British expeditionary force that occupied Cairo in September 1882 and began its slow progress down the Nile early in 1844 in an abortive attempt to rescue Gordon in Khartoum, before being invalided home with the war substantive rank of sergeant. The twins at that time would be only 12½ years old and Bernard approaching sixteen.

If the occasion of Kate's wedding is set aside as being too early a date, it is difficult to find a later occasion to suit the taking of the studio photograph. Perhaps the only feasible occasion would be the wedding of James, say in 1889, but there is no evidence that James married in Manchester at that time. The family tree does not disclose the name of his wife, but does show the year of birth of his first child, Florence Mary, as being 1893, the same year of birth as Patrick's daughter Florence. The possibility of James marrying in Manchester between Kate's marriage and Bernard's emigration cannot be discounted.

However that may be, there can be little doubt that Patrick had kept in close touch with his family in Manchester since his return from active service, and that he and Lucy extended a warm invitation to Molly to come and live with them in Aldershot when the sisters went their various ways.

Kate and Roseanne left the parish of St. Wilfrid in Hulme and went to live in the parish of the Holy Family in Chorlton-on-Medlock. There is no church of that name in Manchester today. In 1908 St. Augustine's church in Granby Row was closed because of vibrations of machinery in the Manchester College of Technology next door. The Manchester City Council agreed to buy the church building in compensation, and the parish of St. Augustine merged with that of the Holy Family. The Holy Family church in York

Street, Chorlton-on-Medlock was renamed St. Augustine's. It was destroyed in an air raid in December 1940. The ruined building was finally demolished in 1966, and the present church of St. Augustine was built on its site.

At the time when the sisters moved to Chorlton-on-Medlock there lived in 95 Tipping Street, Ancoats, a James Finn, traveller; but whether he was their brother James is uncertain.

Kate set up as a dress and mantle maker at 19 St. Saviour Street and Roseanne fell in love.

Her future husband, William Logue, lived at 70 Higher Chatham Street, off Oxford Road. William came from a family of eight children. His mother was the widow of Michael Logue, a saddler by trade, who had died from tuberculosis. William was a rubber vulcaniser by trade.

The year 1894 was eventful for Manchester and for the Finn family. On New Year's Day Queen Victoria came to Manchester to open officially the Manchester Ship Canal to traffic. It was over forty years since she had first visited Manchester with Prince Albert in 1851. Two years after that visit Manchester had been given the status of city. Much had happened in its development in those forty years.

On 7th January 1894, Catherine Finn, widow of old Jack Finn, died of old age in Clooneen. Her son, Thomas of Kiltycreen, was present at her death. It is extremely doubtful whether any of Paddy's children had news of her death. It is equally doubtful whether she had been aware that she had great-grandchildren in Aldershot or grandchildren in America. Clooneen was another time, another place.

On 26th November 1894, William Logue and Roseanne Finn were married at the church of the Holy Family. William was twenty-eight years old. Roseanne's age was given as twenty-one, although she would be twenty-two at the time. Their marriage was witnessed by Roseanne's brother James and by Mary Logue.

Roseanne was living at 14 Cross Street, Chorlton-on-Medlock when she married. After her marriage William and Roseanne Logue set up home in the Manchester district of Rusholme.

In Aldershot Molly also fell in love. There she met and married a serving soldier named Cornelius (Con) Cussen. The groom and Patrick wore dress uniform at the military wedding in the garrison town.

Shortly after Molly's marriage, Patrick received an overseas posting to Malta. Whatever misgivings he and Molly may have had as they recollected their brother John's fatal attack of Malta fever twenty years before, they were quickly overcome by the prospect of a good family life in the Mediterranean station. Patrick was now a warrant officer and there were good family quarters available for Lucy and the children. There was much to recommend the peace-time overseas posting.

Lucy and the children loved the life in Malta. There were jolly parties in the shade of the orange grove. One especially was re-called, a birthday party for Frances which was all but ruined when Patrick's dog Bendigo foraged among the excited children and helped himself to an ample portion of the goodies set aside for the birthday meal.

The halcyon days ended when little Florence contracted fever. It was a comparatively mild attack and she recovered, but Patrick and Andrew were more severely stricken by the disease. Life suddenly became a nightmare for Lucy. Her days were spent caring and fretting over Florence and Billy and visiting the military hospital where Patrick and Andrew were dangerously ill. She was with Patrick when he died, and collapsed at his bedside.

Patrick was given a military funeral. The regimental band was playing the Dead March from Saul as the cortège passed below the windows of the hospital ward where Andrew lay dying. The slow march to the cemetery, the prayers at the graveside and the march back to barracks to the tune of "The Vacant Chair" was a military ceremony in which Lucy was vaguely and tearfully involved.

Patrick was laid to rest, but Lucy's torment continued. Andrew died and there was another funeral to face. This time there was no military music, only the mumbled prayers beside the quietness of the grave and the wrench to the heart as part of it was buried for ever in Malta with husband and son. It was time to return to England with Frances, Billy and Florence.

The year was 1898. That was the year of sadness for Lucy. The preceding year had been so happy. That had been the year of Queen Victoria's Diamond Jubilee and in some strange way the nation had seemed to be rejoicing with the Queen. The poor momentarily forgot their miseries as they joined in the toasts to Queen and Empire, there were fairs and feasts, the children ran home from school with Jubilee mugs in their hands. The privileged were elevated in rank in the Jubilee honours list. Baron Egerton was created Earl Egerton of Tatton and Viscount Salford for his successful chairmanship of the Manchester Ship Canal. And now it was all past, and life had to be faced.

In 1898 both the Finn twins had their first baby. In Manchester Roseanne had a daughter named Gertrude, and in Aldershot Molly had a son named Cornelius (Con) after his father.

Lucy was in a predicament. She did not know whether to return to Molly in Aldershot or to her other sisters-in-law in Manchester. In many ways she was tempted to return to the Hampshire garrison town where she knew people and where the countryside was far more appealing than the smoke-laden streets of Manchester. On the other hand the army had brought much sadness into her life, and being twice widowed she no longer felt part of the garrison community.

After much heart-searching and many misgivings Lucy opted for Manchester. Kate and Roseanne busied themselves settling their sister-in-law and her children to their new life. They found employment for Lucy as housekeeper to the Holy Family presbytery, a position that provided board and lodging for herself, but no accommodation for her children.

Billy went to live with Kate, Frances with Roseanne and Florence with William's mother, "Grandmother" Logue, in Higher Chatham Street. For a time all went well. Billy was shepherded in his new surroundings by Edward, now a boisterous thirteen-year-old extrovert, and by Vincent, a quieter, more introspective boy of seven.

There were many opportunities for Lucy's children to see each other. Lucy made regular visits to St. Saviour's Street with her daughters to see Billy, and Higher Chatham Street was open house to the Logue family. There was much activity and many entertaining evenings when Mrs Logue's children visited the family home. One of her daughters, Margaret, was married to Joe Eliffe who used to sing ballads as they gathered round the piano. These were happy times for little Florence who remembered all her life the words of the ballad she loved best.

> *When the curtains of night are pinned back by the stars,*
> *And the beautiful moon leaves the skies,*
> *When the dewdrops of heaven are kissing the rose,*
> *It is there that my memory flies.*

Florence Finn Highes

Go where you will, by land or by sea,
I will share all your sorrows and cares,
And tonight when I kneel at my bedside and pray,
I'll remember you love in my prayers.

These are the words of the song that Florence loved to hear Joe Eliffe sing, and these are the words she remembered all her life. They were committed to her memory as the permanent representative of all the half-forgotten memories of her childhood days with "Grandmother" Logue.

"She is not your real grandmother," Roseanne once said to her.

Florence burst into tears and Mrs Logue took her in her arms.

"I am your grandmother, my darling," she said, "and always shall be."

The happy fostering of Lucy's children suffered a severe setback over the incident of Billy's shoes.

It arose when one of Lucy's friends told her that she had seen Billy playing barefooted in the school playground. Lucy was aghast. She was used to being commended on how well dressed her children always were, and she was outraged that Kate, who always made sure that Edward and Vincent were properly shod, should allow Billy to go to school without footwear. Barefoot children were a common sight in Manchester in the summer months, but it was an indication of poverty and an offence to respectability.

Lucy confronted Kate with what she regarded as a grave dereliction of duty, and was far from satisfied when Kate told her that Billy was in the habit of taking off his shoes when playing outdoors with barefooted children, and that he had probably forgotten all about them or maybe they had been stolen. Lucy could not believe that Billy would choose to go barefooted, and accused Kate of having stolen the shoes herself, or, which was just as bad, of having pawned them.

Both insinuations outraged Kate. She told Lucy that if she considered her unfit to look after Billy she had better make some new arrangements.

Lucy took her troubles to the presbytery. The parish priest listened sympathetically and offered a solution. He undertook to pay for Billy's education as a boarder at a school run by the Christian Brothers.

"That you will not do, Father," said Lucy. "Not out of the few pennies that are left for you out of the collection plate."

It was finally agreed that she and the priest should each pay half of Billy's school fees. It is possible that the Christian Brothers also contributed by remitting part of the school fees.

So Billy left Manchester to become a boarder at a Lancashire school some miles north of the city. He was sadly missed by Florence, who was more attached to her step-brother than she was to her step-sister, Frances.

Lucy let it be known that Bernard had written to Kate admonishing her for robbing a widow and her poor mites. Roseanne and Molly were unimpressed. To them it was Kate who was the widow and her children the poor mites. They were becoming a little tired of Lucy's airs and graces.

Events soon relegated the family tiff to trivia of the past. In 1899 Molly's second son was born, William John (Bill). On 10th October of that year the country was at war, and an expeditionary force under the command of General Sir Redvers Buller sailed to South Africa. From Aldershot Cornelius Cussen went to war. For Molly, left with her two babies, the far-off war became a grim reality.

In Manchester past differences were healed by time. Lucy and her girls resumed regular visits to 19 St. Saviour Street to see Kate and her boys. Lucy's early prettiness had matured into a maternal beauty. Her black, curly hair had turned white after Patrick's death, but its youthful texture matched her countenance. Kate, on the other hand, had lost most of her youthful spirit and merriment. Lucy's daughters saw her as a quiet, sad-looking woman sitting morosely by her fireside, although she was not yet forty. They never knew Kate as her sisters pictured her.

So the nineteenth century closed with the country at war. Manchester had become a city, the Cottonopolis of England. In 1897, by Treasury Warrant, it was declared a port. Its dockland was being industrialised by the purchase of the 1,200-acre estate of Sir Humphrey de Trafford. Trafford Park became the first industrialised estate in the world, housing the American Westinghouse electrical engineering firm, later to become the English Metropolitan Vickers Company. In 1899 the city enhanced its cultural presence by the building of the John Rylands Library in Deansgate at a cost of £1 million. The library, founded by Lady Rylands in memory of her husband, the foremost cotton manufacturer and textile distributor in the country, contains some of the world's finest literary treasures among its 400,000 books and 12,000 manuscripts. By its industry and culture Manchester had earned its recognition as the capital city of the North of England.

The new century heralded the end of the Victorian age. On 22nd January 1901, Queen Victoria died. Few of her subjects could remember the day of her coronation. It was almost a lifetime ago, back in those distant days when old Jack Finn farmed in Cloontia and Paddy was a small boy. The peaceful countryside of England had erupted in a rash of industry, and the farm workers and their children had gone to the cities to man their workshops, their mills and their warehouses. The cottage industry had almost died. The bounds of Empire had been stretched, and there died that January day not only the Queen of the United Kingdom and its colonies, but also the Empress of India.

In a small degree the new era brought a change of circumstance to the Finn sisters. It was heralded by one of Lucy's now rarer visits to St. Saviour Street with Frances and Florence. They found Kate's house empty and none of the neighbours knew where she and her children had gone.

The reason for Kate's absence from home was that she had gone to live with William and Roseanne Logue in Broadheath on the outskirts of Altrincham, about eight miles south-west of Manchester on the old Roman road to Chester.

Altrincham is an old Cheshire market town of Saxon origin. Its market dates from its charter of 1290 and a three-day fair each year. In 1319 Edward II abolished the three-day fair and replaced it by an annual fair on the feast of St. James, known locally as Sanjam Fair until it was abolished in 1859. When the Finn sisters came to Altrincham Tuesday was still market day and there was much bustle in the town on that day. A new market hall had been built in 1880, the same year that a new railway station had been built in the town centre to replace the original one.

Industry came to Altrincham in the last decade of the nineteenth century. The district of Broadheath on its Manchester side was an ideal area for development. The railway line from Manchester to Liverpool ran through it, and alongside the railway track there was the Bridgewater Canal linking Manchester with Runcorn on the Mersey estuary.

The Bridgewater Canal is the oldest canal in England. It was commissioned by Francis Egerton, 3rd Duke of Bridgewater, and designed by James Brindley. The first phase ran from Worsley to Manchester, to transport coal to the city from the Duke's mines. The savings were so great that the Duke risked his entire capital in extending the canal to Runcorn to transport raw cotton from Liverpool to Manchester. The first phase was completed in 1761 and the second phase in 1795. It established Manchester as the centre of the cotton trade.

The development of Broadheath as an industrial centre occurred in the last decade of the nineteenth century. In 1884 the Oldfield Hall estate came up for sale. A local farmer named Andrew Curtis Sparkes bought about thirty acres on the Altrincham side of the Bridgewater Canal as a speculation. He sold the land to the Lintotype and Machinery Company which used four acres bordering the canal to build spacious offices and workshops. The remaining land was used to build a housing estate for its workers.

William Logue's trade of vulcaniser brought him to Broadheath.

He found work with a firm of rubber manufacturers, Joseph Harris & Son in Viaduct Road, named from the railway viaduct that runs alongside it carrying the railway line over Manchester Road into Broadheath Station.

The Logues came to Broadheath in 1901 and lived at 32 Beaconsfield Road, a small terraced house off Manchester Road quite near Viaduct Road. They spent only about a year in that house before moving into Stamford Terrace on Manchester Road.

About the time of the move Molly came to Broadheath. Her husband, having survived the Boer War, had met his death through scalding when a cauldron of boiling cabbage had accidentally overturned upon him in the field kitchen. Molly was also now a widow with two young children.

Roseanne was pregnant when Molly brought her family to Broadheath. Her second baby was a boy who was baptised and christened William Patrick at St. Vincent's Catholic Church on 4th January 1903.

At that time the church was in New Street. In 1858 the parish priest had bought two old cottages in the street for demolition, and for erection of a church and rectory on the site. By the turn of the century the Catholic population of Altrincham had risen to about 1,700 and the church was too small for its congregation. A site for the present church was found in 1903 in the triangle of land where Bentinck Road and Groby Road merge at the corner of Regent Road.

Molly found a home for herself and her children in a terraced house on the Altrincham side of the Bridgewater canal. Her home at 27 Princes Road faced a plot of waste ground on the perimeter of the Linotype estate now occupied by the Altrincham Ice Rink.

The front room of the house was fitted out as a shop, a not uncommon occurrence in those days, and Molly earned a living by running a small village store from her home. There she met a young man who was soon to become her second husband, an iron turner named Arthur Harman.

The Harmans lived at 11 Norman Road on the Linotype estate. They came from Keighley in Yorkshire, where Arthur's father had been a policeman. He left the police force and made a new career in engineering, and was now a foreman at the Linotype works.

Arthur was a serious young man, and for him it was love at first sight. There were many obstacles to overcome before they could marry. He was eight years or more younger than Molly, and she was a widow with two children. She was also a Catholic, and he was not. Small wonder that his family and friends thought he had lost his head rather than his heart.

Arthur was firm in intent and purpose. He took instruction in the Catholic faith and was received into the Church. He and Molly were married at St. Vincent's Church, New Street, on 11th April 1904 by a young curate named Edward Kirby, who returned to Altrincham some thirty years later as rector of the parish and rural dean. On the marriage certificate Arthur's age was given as twenty-two and Molly's age as twenty-nine, although she would be thirty-one at the time. The certificate was witnessed by William and Roseanne Logue. After they were married Molly and Arthur went to live in Atlantic Street on the Manchester side of the Bridgewater Canal.

That was the year the Logues left Broadheath and moved nearer to the centre of Altrincham. They went to live at 57 Mayors Road, facing Stamford Park. The reason for the move may have been Gertrude's schooling, as Mayors Road is near to St. Vincent's infant school in Hamon Road. The area in which they came to live is known as Hale Moss, which at one time was a stretch of common land where gipsies camped. In 1880 the Earl of Stamford gave the common to Altrincham Council for development. Sixteen acres were landscaped to form Stamford Park, and new roads and houses were built around its perimeter.

It is not known exactly when Kate came to live in Altrincham. She certainly did not move with the Logues when they first came to Broadheath, as Lucy Finn visited them there with her daughters. Florence retained a vivid memory of a railway viaduct being near Roseanne's home although she did not know the name of the road. It is possible that Kate came to live with them after they moved on to Manchester Road. What is certain is that Kate's last home was at 40 Beech Road, Hale, on the opposite side of Stamford Park to her sister.

The ages of Kate's children are relevant to an appraisal of the likely time of her arrival in Altrincham. At the time of Molly's wedding Edward was twenty years old and Vincent was thirteen. There is no evidence that Edward came to Altrincham. Indeed, as will be seen later, there is reason to believe he did not. It is possible that Kate's sole reason for leaving her home in Chorlton-on-Medlock was the prospect of finding employment for Vincent in the rapidly expanding industry in Broadheath when he left school. If this were so, it seems likely that if she stayed with Roseanne at Broadheath it would be for only a short time, and that it is quite possible that she did not come to Altrincham until after the Logues had moved to Mayors Road.

In Altrincham Kate abandoned her business of mantle and dress maker and ran a small shop in Railway Street for the sale of Bibles, missals, prayer books and objects of devotion.

On 18th June 1904 the foundation stone of St. Vincent's new church was laid with due ceremony. The clergy and parishioners assembled outside the New Street church where they were joined by the Mayor of Altrincham in his chain of office, and by the members of the Court Leet and other local dignitaries. They marched in procession to Regent Road, headed by the town band. When the stone was laid it was announced that of the £6,000 needed to build the new church, £2,500 had already been subscribed.

The three Finn sisters were together for only a short time in Altrincham. Molly was the first to leave. Arthur Harman took up employment in Woolwich and the family went to live south of the Thames, east of Woolwich, at 17 Hurst Road, Belvedere, near Erith.

On 2nd July 1905, William and Roseanne's second son was baptised and christened Bernard Joseph in the old church in New Street. In the same year Arthur and Molly had their first baby, a son named Francis Robert.

On 1st October 1905, St. Vincent's new church was consecrated by the Bishop of Shrewsbury.

It was about that time that a family came to Broadheath that was soon to entwine itself among the Finn family tree. Their history had much in common with Paddy's family, although their years in England had not brought such dire consequences.

James Foy was about five years younger than Paddy Finn. He came from County Mayo and was married to Margaret Walsh. He came to England to make his fame and fortune on the music hall stage. It is not known whether he was related to the Lancashire comedian Tom Foy, or for that matter the American Eddie Foy, but he trod the boards with limited success. He was prudent enough, however, to take over the tenancy of a public house in his wife's name. Margaret Foy's public house was the Moulders Arms at 89 Clarendon Street, Hulme. There were no fewer than thirty-one public houses in Clarendon Street in those days. Margaret Foy bore six children whilst managing the Moulders Arms. There were three boys, William, who died as a child, James, and John, the baby of the family who was born in 1900. The three girls were Margaret, Anne and Grace, who was born on 4th November 1891.

The children went to St. Wilfrid's school just as Bernard and the twins had done years before. At home they were subjected to some discipline of restricted entry to the public rooms of the beerhouse, but as they grew older the piano in the concert room became an irresistible attraction. Margaret quickly learned to play. She had a good ear for music and at an early age she could play the popular songs of the day. She found herself in popular demand in the concert room under the watchful eye of her mother.

In the first decade of the twentieth century twelve public houses in Clarendon Street were closed on the grounds of unsuitability or non-requirement, including the Moulders Arms. James Foy anticipated the inevitable. He abandoned his stage career and got a job as storekeeper at the Linotype works. He took his wife and family, and the pub piano from Clarendon Street, and they went to live at 103 Lawrence Road on the Linotype estate. Grace Foy was almost fourteen when they moved to Broadheath. Ten years later she married Vincent Glover.

In June 1906, William Grey, Ninth Earl of Stamford, left New-foundland and crossed the Atlantic to take up residence at Dunham Hall, the family seat. He was born in Newfoundland in 1850 and succeeded to the title in 1890.

The Grey family trace their lineage to Henry VIII. His great-granddaughter, Lady Jane Grey, daughter of the Duke of Suffolk, was proclaimed Queen of England after the death of Edward VI. After a reign of only nine days, she was ousted by Mary Tudor and executed six months later with her husband, Lord Guildford Dudley.

Altrincham was bedecked with flags and bunting as its people lined the streets to welcome the homecoming earl. He drove through the town with his wife and their two children, Roger and Jane, in an open horse-drawn landau driven by two liveried coachmen. The earl wore a grey frock coat and top hat. His wife and daughter were dressed in white, and young Roger wore a boater, a long-sleeved white shirt with tie, and white shorts that covered his knees.

At Dunham the local dignitaries attended the reception held on the lawn in front of the Hall. A marquee had been erected and from its gable a line of bunting stretched to the nearby trees of the deer-park. As the landau approached the Hall, top hats, derbies and boaters were raised to greet the lord of the manor and his family.

There was also a more personal rejoicing that year in the Logue family following the birth of William and Roseanne's third son, Michael Francis (Mike). It was also a year of anxiety for them. William lost his job as a vulcaniser, and as there was no work to be found in his trade he took up employment as agent for the Prudential Assurance Company. The job consisted of the collection of weekly payments of whole life insurance whereby the subscriber could insure himself, his wife and his children for as little as a penny per head to provide sufficient funds at death to meet funeral expenses. As that was its main purpose the insurance was known colloquially as the "Death and Burial Club". It was about the time of change of occupation that the Logues left Altrincham and went to live in the Stockport area.

In 1907 the first electric tramcar was to be seen in Altrincham. The canal bridge at Broadheath was widened to cope with the increasing traffic to and from the engineering works. The new tramway between Altrincham and Manchester was opened for public use and the route was lined with sightseers as the double-deck tram, with open verandahs and spiral staircases, began its journey from the foot of the Downs. Its first stop was at the junction of Regent Road and George Street, just before Kate's shop. But Kate was not there to witness the historic event. She was terminally ill with cancer of the stomach.

Molly travelled from Belvedere to be with her sister, and was with her when she died at 40 Beech Road on 3rd July 1907. William Logue bought the plot for her grave in Altrincham and Hale Cemetery, and she was buried there on 6th July.

When their mother died, Edward Glover was aged twenty-two and Vincent was sixteen. As there is no evidence of Edward's presence either from the death certificate or the cemetery register, it must be assumed that he had left the area and may have been unaware of his mother's death. Since the departure from Manchester the whole family seems to have lost track of him.

William and Roseanne completed their family the year after Kate died with the birth of their second daughter, Monica Rose. Life had become more difficult since William had lost his job as vulcaniser, and Roseanne was finding it harder to budget the limited house-keeping to meet the needs of their growing family. Letters from Bernard encouraged them to emigrate and start a new life in America, but the thought of arriving in a strange country with five young children deterred them.

In 1910 Arthur and Molly Harman's first child was born, a daughter named Winifred.

The following year William and Roseanne Logue succumbed to Bernard's entreaties. They embarked on a cargo boat bound for Philadelphia in search of a more rewarding life for themselves and their children.

Three years later England was at war. The Great War, as it became called, began with Austria-Hungary declaring war on Serbia on 28th July 1914, following the assassination of the Archduke Francis Ferdinand and his wife at Sarajevo on 28th June. On 1st August Germany declared war on Russia. On 3rd August Germany sent an ultimatum to Belgium. On 4th August Britain declared war.

Molly's eldest son Con was sixteen the year war broke out. He overstated his age and enlisted. In 1916 he became victim of a poison gas attack and was invalided home.

Lucy's son Billy Owen enlisted in the navy and horrified his mother when he told her that he would still be serving on mine-sweeping duties after the armistice. He survived unscathed.

Arthur Harman worked as an adviser to the Ministry of Munitions in the layout of a machine-gun factory.

Vincent Glover, an iron miller by trade, was living at 49 Middles-brough Road, Coventry, when he returned to Altrincham to marry Grace Foy at St. Vincent's church on 18th November 1915. He later went to Crayford, south of the Thames near Dartford, to work in an aeroplane factory.

After the war Arthur Harman bought an old thatched cottage in three acres of land so that Con, who was advised to lead an outdoor life, could run a poultry farm. They called the cottage "Clooneen".

They returned to Manchester in the late 1920s and were living in Ravenswood Road, Old Trafford, in March 1930 when Grace Glover visited them after Vincent's death. They then had two children at home, Cecilia, born in 1912, and Arthur, born in 1914. Winifred had become a Carmelite nun and was in a convent in Reading.

PADDY FINN'S CHILDREN

Fom Manchester they went to live in Coventry, where Molly died in 1939. She was a small, sweet woman of gentle nature, capable of singing Irish rebel songs at the kitchen sink. With her death the story of Paddy's children in England is, as far as is known, all but complete. The rest of the story unfolds across the Atlantic Ocean.

America

Paddy was probably not the only son of Jack Finn to leave Ireland. Bernard recalled hearing of an uncle who deserted his wife and sixteen children, went to America and was never heard of again. Then there was an uncle in Australia who sent him money for his passage there, but family finances were so bad in Manchester at the time that Bernard handed the money over to Kate to augment the housekeeping. He later repaid the Australian uncle. There was also the father of the cousin in Cincinnati. Any one of them could, of course, have been Mary Hannon's brother, but in 1939 a James Francis Finn was unearthed in Colorado Springs whose family came from near Clooneen.

Tom was the first of Paddy's children to cross the Atlantic. He emigrated soon after his father's death when the family was in dire need. His sense of responsibility towards his sisters contrasts adversely with that of Bernard, who forfeited his first opportunity to emigrate. After Paddy's death, Tom's consuming desire was to emigrate, and that he achieved.

There is no indication that he met up with any relative in America, and initially he must have had a hard time. Irish labour was not welcomed by the American community at large. It could be hired cheaply and so tended to lower the general rate of pay. Tom found work on the railroad, and when Bernard joined him he was fireman on an engine engaged in hauling ballast and a gang of trackmen laying crushed rock on the railway track between Fort Scott and Parsons, Kansas.

Bernard Finn embarked on the Cunard liner *Servia* on 28th February 1890. Barney Finn disembarked at New York on 9th March, two days after his twenty-first birthday. Bernard chose to call himself Barney, and that is the name he will bear from now on.

Once ashore he had to register as an alien. That done he exchanged his remaining sterling for US dollars, had his first bite to eat on American soil from a loaf of rye bread tasting of garlic, and then booked a roundabout rail route from New York to Fort Scott via Cincinnati to visit his cousin. He could have saved himself the additional fare. His reception was frigid and he was soon back on Cincinnati railway station awaiting a train to take him to Fort Scott. He had only a few dollars left and was depressed close to tears. As he boarded the train he consoled himself with the thought that he had a brother at Fort Scott and a new life ahead.

Barney travelled day and night in a coach reeking of tobacco smoke, and eventually reached Fort Scott on 15th March. Tom did not come to the station to meet him, and he had to find his way to the hotel where Tom was staying and await his brother there. At last Tom arrived with his engineer, Jack Sheehan. He was ten years older than Barney, had grown a moustache since leaving England, and looked a man to be reckoned with. Tom gave his younger brother a perfunctory welcome such as any recently nationalised American citizen might bestow on any Irish alien who claimed his acquaintance. He showed little interest in Barney's future. After all the encouraging words in Tom's letters this second rebuff made Barney sick at heart. He remembered Kate's remark before Tom emigrated. "Fine words butter no parsnips, Tom."

It was left to Jack Sheehan to persuade John Fallon, the gang foreman, to give Barney a job as trackman. Shortly afterwards, Tom and Sheehan were transferred to Hannibal. Tom left without even wishing Barney good luck. Barney worked with the gang for three months, his blistered hands gradually hardening to the work of tamping ties and shovelling rock. By June the ballast work was coming to an end and Barney submitted his resignation.

"Barney, you weren't worth a damn when I first gave you a job," John Fallon told him as he accepted the resignation, "but after a while you became as good as most of the men. Anyhow, you don't belong here and I hope you find work to your liking elsewhere. Since your brother is running out of Hannibal I suggest you go there."

At Hannibal, Barney approached the foreman of the locomotive repair shed and was given night work at the cinder pit at the rate of 1.25 dollars a night, seven nights a week. The hard work gave him added strength and weight — he now weighed twelve-and-a-half stone. Whilst there he was selected to act as relief fireman on a local freight train bound for Sidelia, about 160 miles away. Shortly afterwards he was transferred to New Franklin to fire a leaky old switch engine at the junction. From that job he advanced to regular fireman on a line colloquially referred to as the "Snake Route" as the track followed a snakelike course as it wound alongside the banks of the Missouri River.

He was firing a heavy work engine on that route when high waters caused landslides on the track and washed out bridges, preventing the train from returning to base. The crew was marooned for about three weeks, after which time Barney was hospitalised in Sedalia with fever, a condition that returned each summer for from one to three weeks with montonous regularity.

One summer, after the annual bout of fever, the hospital doctor discharged him with a new remedy.

"Barney," he told him, "here is an old woman's prescription which you may take without fear of injury. Every morning before breakfast take a tablespoonful of raw cornmeal and shake it up in a goblet of water, then drink it."

Barney took the cornmeal as directed. He never suffered chills or fever again. When next he met the doctor, Barney told him how effective the remedy had been. The doctor laughed and replied, "It works, or seems to, on some. On others it has no effect at all."

Barney enjoyed life in New Franklin. He took board and lodging in the home of George Edwards, a Justice of the Peace, who helped him to get his first declaration of citizenship from the county clerk at Fayette. He was exuberant and parodied the libretto of *HMS Pinafore* as he sang:

> He is American
>   For he himself has said it,
>   And it's greatly to his credit
> That he is American.
> For he might have been a Rooshian,
> French or Turk or Prooshian
>   Or perhaps Ital-ian.
> But in spite of all temptations
>   To belong to other nations
>   He became AMERICAN.

Whilst in New Franklin he joined the railway trades union, the Brotherhood of Locomotive Firemen, and became secretary of the New Franklin lodge. In this capacity he assisted his brother Tom who had injured his shoulder and applied for discharge from employment and a total disability allowance of 1,500 dollars. Barney pleaded Tom's case successfully, but in doing so made enemies of some lodge members who suspected nepotism.

Tom invested his disability allowance in a saloon and brothel in the red light district of Sedalia. When Barney visited him there, Tom showed his gratitude by offering him any girl in the place. Barney was unimpressed.

Tom enjoyed his new enterprise for only a year or two. He fell foul of the Sedalia underworld and was murdered. Like the assailant who shot at him and his father years before from the hedgerow at Frenchpark, the murderer was never caught. Tom's body was buried in the Catholic cemetery outside Sedalia.

Barney settled Tom's affairs, paid off some of his debts, quarrelled with an outstanding creditor, and emerged badly out of pocket.

After seven years working on the railroad Barney fired his last engine in 1897. Firemen were paid by mileage run at the rate of 2½ cents a mile. His monthly wage varied between sixty and eighty-five dollars. To run the mileage required to earn eighty-five dollars necessitated his averaging only four hours sleep a day during that month. Nevertheless, after working as regular fireman for six years he had saved 1,500 dollars, the equivalent of Tom's disability allowance. He too had decided to go into business for himself.

About the time when Barney was contemplating leaving the railway his brother Edward emigrated to the Argentine Republic. Edward had married a girl named Carolyn Botley. They had two daughters. The elder was named Violet. The younger, born in 1894, was named Marie Rose, but Edward nicknamed her Trilby because, as she was a small baby, her bootees were always coming off. Her constant barefootedness reminded Edward of Trilby in Gerald du Maurier's novel who, as an artists' model, bared her feet so that art students could sketch them. Edward went to Argentina whilst Trilby was still a baby. He may have been prompted to seek a life out there from visits whilst in the Royal Marines. In any event he left his family in England whilst he established himself and found a home for them there.

Edward met with an accident in his early days in Argentina. He was riding through cattle-grazing country in the Santa Fé area leading a spare horse when one of the horses caught its foot in an entrance hole of a viscacha burrow. Edward was thrown and badly dislocated his shoulder. He was carried over the cattle lands for three days in a semi-conscious state before reaching a doctor.

Carolyn and their two daughters joined him shortly afterwards and the family settled down in their adopted country. They had four more children, two sons, Terry and Fred, and a third daughter named Pat, followed by a third son named Jack. When Jack was still a baby the family returned to England for some reason, and the eldest daughter, Violet, became a hospital nurse. They were in England in 1912 when Carolyn's mother, grandma Botley, died. They returned to Argentina shortly afterwards when Pat was ten years old.

Edward found his metier in Argentina when he started to earn his living by writing for an English language newspaper in Buenos Aires. The newspaper press was to be the livelihood of of both Edward and Barney.

Barney entered the newspaper world almost by chance when, through the Edwards family, he met Arthur Rozelle, publisher of a newspaper in Lamar, Missouri. Rozelle thought that Barney showed talent as a writer and suggested that he might profitably invest his savings and start a new career by buying the *Farm Record*, a newspaper published in Ava, Missouri, and now up for sale. On balance it appears that Rozelle may have been looking after the newspaper proprietor's interests rather than Barney's in proposing that a twenty-eight-year-old railway fireman should invest in a business about which he knew nothing, but Barney was not deterred, despite the fact that he was in sight of promotion from fireman to engineer. He went to Ava and arranged the purchase at an agreed price of 850 dollars.

Having embarked on a rash commercial adventure, Barney compounded his recklessness by deciding it was time he got married. The object of his affection was Henrietta Klineline, the seventeen-year-old daughter of Henry Klineline, former sheriff and collector of the county. Barney came across his future father-in-law one day when Henry Klineline was discussing politics with two friends. As he approached he chanced to overhear their conversation.

"Klineline," one was saying, "you can't vote for that man running on your Democratic ticket for sheriff."

"Why not?" asked Klineline.

The third man in the trio thereupon interjected, "Why, you know as well as I do that he's a son of a bitch."

Edward Finn in Buenos Aires, Argentina

"Yes, I know that and more," answered Klineline. "But how about your man running on your ticket?"

"Well," said the first, "there's no denying that he's also a son of a bitch."

"All right," said Klineline, "you fellows go and vote for your son of a bitch, and I'll vote for mine."

Barney concluded that Henry Klineline's political philosophy, while crudely stated, was about as good as any observed in practical politics. The next time they met, Barney asked for Henrietta's hand in marriage. Consent was given, and a simple wedding without frills was arranged for 21st January 1898, two weeks and three days before Henrietta's eighteenth birthday. They were to be happily married for over fifty-seven years.

Barney made no profit from the *Farm Record*, but he gained a wealth of experience. A Democratic paper in a predominantly Republican county had little chance of success in the hands of a novice. But he quickly learned the ploys and skulduggery of the newspaper business, sometimes to his cost.

For instance, one day he met a one-armed man named Crane who told him that if he went upstairs in the Miller block he would find something to put in the paper. Eager for copy, Barney walked over to the Miller block. As he climbed the stairs he met a friend coming downstairs who appeared embarrassed at their meeting. At the top of the stairs a slatternly looking woman stood in an open doorway. She leered at him and invited him inside. Barney declined and went back to the office. That week's issue of the Republican newspaper, the *Douglas County Herald*, bore the following challenge under a black headline: "Stand up Barney Finn and answer this question. Did or didn't you meet a disreputable woman in the Miller building by appointment last Monday?"

To safeguard himself against actions arising from the written word, such as libel, Barney decided to study law. He rather surprised himself by passing the Bar examination, but he never practised. He advised anybody who sought his counsel to avoid litigation if at all possible.

Early in the spring of 1899 Barney received a letter from a Mrs Joseph Vaughn informing him that there was an opening for a newspaper in her home town, Sarcoxie, as fire had destroyed the type and machinery of the newspaper run by her family. Barney made the journey to Sarcoxie in mid-May, and liked what he saw.

The strawberry season was at its peak. Refrigerator cars at the rail depot were receiving strawberry crates by the wagonload. Horse traders swarmed around the town square.

It took two years for Barney to establish himself in Sarcoxie. He disposed of the Ava *Farm Record*, auctioned his household chattels, loaded his printing equipment on wagons and moved to Sarcoxie, one of the oldest towns in Missouri. He set up his Chicago Stop Cylinder press over the Horton & Barbee grocery store on the south side of the town square, and on the 2nd August 1901 issued the first number of his paper, the *Record.*

He was thankful for all the newspaper experience he had gained in Ava, but more than that, he had found there a loyal and sympathetic wife ready to share the troubles along with the joys of their life in Sarcoxie for many years to come. This was the town where for the first time in his life he felt welcome as a valued addition to a kindly, old-fashioned community that considered people living within a fifteen-mile radius as friends and neighbours.

Henrietta was pregnant when they moved to Sarcoxie and they were soon to celebrate the birth of their first child, a son named Bernard Lee (Lee). They were happy days. To help him run the paper Barney took on a youth with a crippled leg, named Fred Erke. Fred was loyal and industrious and within a few years was to prove his worth.

In 1906 Barney almost succumbed to a desire to abandon the newspaper business and return to railroading. The reason was a fire which destroyed most of the printing plant, including the Chicago Stop Cylinder press. Friends saved much of the type and machinery and when Barney arrived to inspect the damage the salvage was spread out in the street. The sight made him sick at heart and ready to quit, but Fred Erke raised his spirits by reminding him that they had a Washington hand press that would suffice until such time when a more up-to-date press could be purchased.

That year Barney had been nominated by the Democrats for the office of probate judge. In the conflagration one thousand El Toro cigars intended for the electors went up in smoke. Barney was defeated by a small margin. Barney regretted his defeat at the time and wondered whether the El Toro cigars would have saved the day. He later regarded the defeat as a salutary warning not to mix the newspaper business with politics. He soldiered on with the *Record* with the help of Fred Erke and the Washington hand press.

The following year Barney accepted an offer to work in Texas as a reporter on the El Paso *Times*. Henrietta was showing symptoms of what could be tuberculosis, and the therapy of a change of climate weighed heavily in favour of acceptance. So the Finns journeyed south-west to where the Rio Grande flows down from the San Andres mountains and skirts Texas on the Mexican border. The work there was so different from Barney's routine that he could not settle and fretted about how Fred Erke was coping with the *Record* in Sarcoxie. Both he and Henrietta admitted to being homesick, and after a short time he relinquished the post.

When they returned to Missouri Henrietta was obviously pregnant, to the delight and merriment of their friends and neighbours who would cheerfully greet Barney in the street with, "Hello, Barney, when do you intend to go to Texas again for your wife's health?"

The baby, a daughter named Margaret, was born on 18th January 1908. Barney soon nicknamed her "Torchy" because of her flaming red hair. As a young child she would sit on his knee as he told her Irish folk tales of the little people, stories that Martin Millmow had told him when he was a little boy in Clooneen. Because he was also interested in astronomy, he would tell her stories about the constellations, pointing out to her Job's Coffin and the Seven Sisters, one of whom he said had her light dimmed because she fell in love with a mortal.

Barney and Henrietta had just moved house to their new home near the top of the steep hill from the town square when the Logues arrived in America. They had crossed the Atlantic by cargo boat and landed at Philadelphia on St. Patrick's Day, 17th March 1911. Barney was there to meet them. It was twenty-one years since he and Roseanne had seen each other.

Roseanne was a girl of seventeen when Barney last saw her in Manchester. Now she was a married woman with five children. There were many introductions to be made and much to talk about. There was plenty of time for both on the long train journey to Missouri. As the train sped south through day and night, Roseanne became frightened. She could not imagine a train could travel so far without hurtling them all into the sea.

At Sarcoxie, Henrietta was busily preparing for the immigrants' arrival. Part of the upstairs rooms in the new house was not yet completed and she converted the space into a dormitory for the

Logue children. Lee and Margaret eagerly awaited the arrival of their English cousins, but when they arrived they might have come from another world. They dressed differently and their flat north country English dialect contrasted strangely with their own Missouri drawl.

There was some consternation when it was discovered that Gertrude had picked up head lice en route. Each day the scalps of the children of both families were thoroughly examined and their hair fine-tooth combed until Henrietta and Roseanne were satisfied all were clear. Any louse discovered was immediately extracted and dunked in kerosene.

William Logue found work as a mechanic at the tramways depot in Springfield, Missouri. He later took a job in the Springfield railway sheds. For the first few years the family lived in rented accommodation, then they bought their first house at 1320 Frisco Avenue, Springfield. They added an extra bedroom and a front porch, of which they were very proud. After the war they bought another house in a much more desirable location, 1233 North Clay Avenue, to which they added two more bedrooms. The house had a large front garden in which grew three giant maple trees. The front yard and the front porch became the family's pride and joy.

Barney and Henrietta completed their family in 1916 with the birth of their second son, named John Franklin but always known as Pat. As his children grew, Barney dreamed his dreams of them, of Sarcoxie, and of his newspaper. His dreams, like so many nebulous wishes, remained unfulfilled. As a leading citizen of Sarcoxie, being elected mayor three times, he hoped the town would develop into a county seat and thereby enhance the importance and revenue of his newspaper. Instead, Carthage was made county seat and Sarcoxie remained the small, friendly community that in many ways time passed by. Alongside his hopes for the town he envisaged himself as head of a group of newspapers with each of his children managing one. But very few are granted the power to create a dynasty, and one by one his children went their own way. They, like Barney, were determined to lead their own lives.

The joy of the Logue famly in their new home proved to be transitory. Three years after the move to North Clay Avenue, Roseanne died. Her death was followed two years later, in 1924, by that of Gertrude. By that time the Logue boys were grown up and making their way in the world. The youngest, Michael (Mike), graduated from high school that year and started work at Reps Drygoods Store where he had worked temporarily after school hours and on Saturdays whilst at high school. In 1926 he had a year in Chicago at the Koester School of Merchandising, after which he felt well qualified to tackle anything in commerce. He had not allowed for the world depression that followed the Wall Street crash, but found a niche in Corning, New York State, in 1928. There he met Catherine (Kay) Parker.

Mike and Kay were married in 1930, the same year that his eldest brother William married Leola German. Monica, the youngest of the family, married John Duane from St. Louis, Missouri, the following year, and moved to Houston, Texas, shortly afterwards. The remaining brother, Bernard Joseph (Barney), married Mary Murphy in 1933, the year that their father, William Logue, died.

The children of William and Roseanne were all born in England. By fortune, and the persuasion of Barney Finn, they were reared in America. That became their parents' homeland, their own home-land, and their children's homeland. They yearned for no other.

Barney Finn's dream of a group of newspapers, each managed by one of his children, was nourished as he watched his son Lee growing up. The days were past when Lee squatted in his tree-house and denied entry to his tomboy little sister Margaret. To her the tree-house was forbidden territory, just as Michael's bush had been to Barney in the faraway world of Clooneen. Lee advanced from high school to the University of Missouri College of Journalism and from there to the Columbia University in New York, but he did not finish college, nor did he found a provincial newspaper under the aegis of Barney. Instead he moved into a highly successful marketing career culminating in the formation of his own advertising firm in New York City. He married Marabeth Storrs and they had three children, Mary Lee, Bernard ("Boo") and Margaret ("Kiki").

When Lee was starting his career his sister Margaret was still a schoolgirl. Her high school friends called her Jack, short for Jumping Jack, because she was jumping centre on the school basketball team. But her real love was dramatics. Barney was a popular public speaker and he would take her along to chautauqua meetings where she gave monologues. She also acted in school plays. From high school she went to Carthage Junior College, with some financial assistance from Lee in the form of a loan which she

A summer afternoon in Sarcoxie, Missouri
(Lee, Margaret, Henrietta, Pat, and Barney Finn.)

later repaid. Her major was dramatics. Then one summer vacation she had the opportunity of acting in the legitimate theatre at Martha's Vineyard. But Barney would have none of it. He said he would never speak to her again if she went. Margaret returned home, her dramatic aspirations thwarted.

In about 1928 Margaret met a young man named Clyde Corwin Moyer. Clyde had come to Sarcoxie to open a restaurant for the profitable strawberry-picking season. He was staying with his brother Claud who had the Ford agency there. For the time being the romance was as ephemeral as the strawberry season. Clyde left to work in Aruba, an island in the Netherlands Antilles off the north coast of Venezeula. Margaret became engaged to someone else, but the engagement was broken off when Clyde reappeared. Perhaps remembering Barney's veto to her acting career, Margaret was taking no chances. The reunited pair eloped and were married in Clyde's brother Lon's home in Stockton, Missouri. That was in 1932 when, as man and wife, they left Missouri for Aruba.

Margaret Finn and William Finn Moyer

Barney's hopes of a newspaper dynasty faded as he watched his youngest child, Pat, grow up. Pat was a rough and tumble boy, ready to have a go at anything. He was an avid collector. Among his collections were Indian arrow-heads, wasps' nests and shot-off dynamite caps. A glimpse of him as a young schoolboy is contained in a letter Barney wrote to Lee in 1927 after he was married.

> "Your mother-in-law sent a Zulu shield to Pat with two other pretty things for Margaret, and your brother whooped like a Zulu when he received his gift. He has had a great grief. A week or so ago he brought home a tadpole with some minnows from the creek, placing them in a wash-boiler. Day by day he watched the tadpole absorb its tail and make progress towards being a bullfrog. When the metamorphosis was about complete he placed a fragment of board in the tub and on this the froggie climbed. Along came dire Fate in the form of a young rooster, which ate the frog. The Missus says that Pat's cries could be heard for at least two blocks. I had told him he should take the fish and frog back to their natural habitat, but he did not heed. After the calamity, as is usual in such cases, he put the minnows in a can and took them back to the creek."

Pat was the only one of Barney's children to complete four full years at college. He graduated from the Colorado School of Mines with a degree in petroleum engineering and went on to work for the Standard Oil Company of Indiana. His brother-in-law, Clyde Moyer, worked for the Standard Oil Company of New Jersey, as later did Clyde's two brothers, Claud and Lon.

He married Irene Wooten from Sarcoxie whilst at college and they had two daughters, Sheila and Nancy. His work took him abroad to Argentina, Iran, Egypt and Libya, and to such places in the States as Little Buffalo Basin, Wyoming, which his wife averred had two seasons, winter and the fourth of July.

So Barney's dream of involving his children in an expanding newspaper business ended, but life was good. He was a leading citizen of Sarcoxie and was elected mayor on three occasions. His keen intellect and sense of humour made him a popular public speaker. Through his newspaper, his official duties and public utterances he influenced the progress of the community. His wife, strong-willed and intelligent herself, was devoted to him. His children grew up healthy and successful.

Henrietta fed him well, although he was not a big eater. She raised squash, corn, tomatoes, carrots and stringbeans in profusion, and kept an enclosed yard full of chickens. In summer she put on a big floppy hat and went out to the nearby farms early in the morning to pick strawberries, which she put in a big bowl on the kitchen table with a bowl of sugar alongside. In season she made delicious peach cobblers and apple pies. There were always plenty of new-laid eggs, and fried chicken was a standard main course.

Barney lived simply. Each morning he rose early, got himself a bowl of oatmeal and had a quiet breakfast before facing the day's work. He usually wore baggy woollen trousers, held up by a pair of wide braces, a shirt with an oversize collar and either a grey woollen cardigan or a dark jacket. On his head he wore a golfer's little peaked cap. Thus attired he strolled down the hill to the town square, greeting his friends on the way. At the newspaper he turned his hand to everything from loading the linotype to writing the editorial for the Thursday issue. After the paper had gone to press he would resume the cycle of collecting news items and sale of advertising space to the local tradesmen.

In summertime he snatched a few hours now and then to take his old fly rod to the nearby stream and fish for perch or bass. On a fine summer evening he would take a hoe and rake and potter around Henrietta's garden, or just sit beneath the shade of a large tree. Some evenings he would take to his small room at the top of the stairs and read a book or write. When the evenings shortened he would sometimes fall asleep in an easy chair by the cabinet radio, and the still of the twilight would be broken by his loud snores and the drone of the radio. On such occasions not even Lord Egerton in his library at Tatton or warming his stockinged feet by the hotel fire at Buxton was more content nor more in control of the world around him than was Barney Finn. The day ended for Barney soon after nine o'clock. Then he would undress, put on his nightshirt and nightcap and retire for the night.

Throughout the years Barney kept up a spasmodic correspondence with his brother Edward in Buenos Aires, encouraged no doubt by their mutual interest in the written word as a source of pleasure and a means of livelihood. To their children they were "Uncle Ned" and "Uncle Ben". The essence of a letter written to

Barney by Edward's daughter Trilby in 1941, when Edward was seventy-six and Barney seventy-two, throws so much light on Edward's family that it merits transcription in full.

Juramento 3028,
Buenos Aires.
13th August, 1941

Dear Uncle Ben,

I really think it is about time I answered your charming letter of — I am ashamed to think how long ago — and to thank you for the cuttings. I loved your little poem and am glad your ideas take that line. Where you are diffident, though, I am confident. I spurned "faith" with youthful audacity at the age of fifteen and proudly announced myself an atheist until nearly forty, when I accidentally came across a new line of thought, studied it thoroughly, found it made sense of what I had concluded was nonsense, gave me a new slant on life, and death, did not restore "faith", but gave me knowledge and a perfect trust in the ultimate strength of the City of Mansoul, however much it may be rocking at present. So that is what you call my "philosophy" uncle, but it is more than that, as it has a concrete foundation, which is more than faith built on mere religious creed and dogma can boast. I also know there are ghosts and fairies, neither of which I believed in as a child. There is certainly fun in growing old when one finds the most interesting lessons are left to the last in the school of life.

Since you seem interested in my name I will divulge the great secret. It is really Marie Rose, but I was nicknamed "Trilby" after George du Maurier's famous character, which saw the light in publication about the same as I did, 1894, by Dad, owing to the fact that I was a very wee baby and no little booties would stay on my feet. Hence I was almost constantly barefooted like my namesake, who was an artist's model for the feet if you remember.

We were all so sorry to hear of your illness. Our sympathy is very acute since Fred, brother number two, is suffering from the same trouble; in fact a good 75% of the menfolk here have duodenum upset in some form or other. B.A. is notorious for its effect on the innards, though nobody can tell why.

Fred is going to an American doctor, who has promised to fix him up. Straighten him out were his exact, and slightly ominous words. I don't know what the treatment will be, as he hasn't got beyond the diagnosing stage yet, but if he can make poor old Fred less green of countenance, that will be at least something. I do hope you will stick to the prescribed diet for the necessary period, and not indulge in a desperate orgy of pickles and canned products with a view to varying the monotony. Get your family to muzzle you if you feel that kind of attack coming on. We know people who have been completely cured after a martyrdom of the prescribed diet, so keep your chin up and the mush down.

Dad is looking considerably better now, and is much more cheerful. It is such a pity he is so deaf. A friend of ours, who is a medium, told us her medical guide had informed her that Dad's deafness was due to a fall from his horse many years ago, and lack of medical attention at the time had resulted in the blood and pus becoming clogged in the passage to the ear. This set up an irritation which over the years caused deafness. She said she was shown a picture of an old woman mixing *yuyus* (herbs) in a bowl and applying them to his injury. Now this was certainly good evidence as the medium, Mrs Randall, was on a social visit to us, not professionally, and had never seen Dad nor heard anything about him in her life before. She seemed to like him, however, and was sorry for and curious about his deafness. So she said she would speak quietly to her guide, closed her eyes and told us what I have written.

Now Dad did have a fall from his horse, roughly about 45 years ago, when he was living out in the camp — Santa Fé I believe it was. We, of course, were in England, and I a baby. He was leading another horse, and either that or his own caught its foot in the opening to a viscacha and fell. Dad was dragged from his horse and badly dislocated his shoulder. I understand it was three days' trek over the camp, presumably on horseback, before a doctor could be reached. He didn't remember anything about an old woman, but he was semi-conscious most of the time. He did remember, however, that he was carried to some sort of estancia, and no doubt it was there that the old woman mixed her *yuyus*. You can imagine that almost anything can be started by a mishap like that, and

I have no doubt whatever that Mrs Randall's guide was right. She was about to suggest some treatment with rays, etc., when she suddenly stopped and said quietly, "They are telling me not to trouble him with anything like that, as he has not much longer to go. He is very tired and one day he will go to bed and not wake up again. You will find him asleep. We are all very proud of the courage he has shown and will all be waiting to welcome him."

After that she gave us a whole list of names of people who were connected with Dad (old family names she told us) who would be there to greet him. I can't remember them all, but there was a Thomas, a James and a Mary ("Tell him I am the one with the dress with the big flounces" was her message) and a Laura. (I believe Dad had an old sweetheart named Laura.) I don't think Dad heard much of what she was saying, so we only passed on to him as much as we thought judicious. He didn't make any comment, so I cannot say what he thought. I am just passing this on for your information and, possibly, interest.

Mrs Randall has since left for England, but promised to write to us if she ever received any information that affected Dad or us, or any message from our little Mother. We are terribly sorry to lose her as she was our connecting link with Mummie, but on the other hand mediums are badly needed at home and she thought it her duty to go. The last we heard of Mummie was that she was perfectly well and happy. When she made her first effort to speak to us she was still feeling very weak and ill, but that has all gone now and she is splendid. She says she cried when she first realised that the parting had come, but was soon shown that she could be with us just the same, and that made everything perfect. She seemed to know of Pat's new house, even to the little pond in the garden. She says she will try to show herself to Carol, Pat's little daughter. She did try to show herself to Violet but was not successful for reasons which Vi, as a medium, knows. Vi is a natural medium, but does not practise.

At one time she quite involuntarily went into a trance and was clairvoyant, clairaudient and receptive to automatic writing, but she gave it up to study further as she wishes to develop healing capability. Jack and Pat share her gift of clairvoyance.

Vi once saw a ghost of the living, long before she had heard of spiritualism. She saw her old sweetheart waiting for her outside the hospital in England where she was nursing. She hurried over to him, forgetting that he was at that time in Borneo working on a rubber plantation. When she realised it he disappeared. Long afterwards he went to the Great War. That was the last we heard of him until about two months ago when his spirit told Pat that he had been shot in France and drowned in a water-filled shell-hole. I suppose that when Vi saw him he was having one of his attacks of malaria and had involuntarily projected his astral body to England.

Pat saw a ghost of the dead soon after we arrived in this country the last time. She was then only ten, and knew even less than we about spiritualism. Small brother Jack had just burst into her bedroom to tell her that there was a roof to the house which you could go in. Although both were born here they were babies when we left and knew nothing of *azateas* as the patio roofs are called. As she scrambled out of bed and put on her socks, Pat saw a sort of cloud at the foot of the bed and out of that strange cloud on that bright sunny morning there came the form of Grannie (Mummie's mother, greatly loved by us all, who had passed on in 1912). She just looked at Pat, smiled with a slight inclination of the head, then disappeared. Pat was puzzled, but too interested about the roof to give it much thought. She didn't tell Mummie until some time later.

One would think it should have been Mummie to whom her mother appeared to welcome her to the new country, but Mummie wasn't mediumistic in the least, so it would have been wasted energy. You cannot ring up people direct unless they have a telephone. You have to go to someone else who has . . .

Let me see, you wanted to know a few details about us. We are not an outstanding crowd, but here is a summary.

Violet Very charming, medium sized, dark hair and eyes. Very like Mummie. Very gay, serene and a perfectly inspired nurse. Housekeeping when not studying psychics.

Trilby Not a bit charming; five foot nothing, studious but lazy. Secretary to Management of Frigorifico Anglo these last twenty years. At present wasting the company's valuable time writing to her Uncle Ben. Dark, cropped hair and dark eyes.

Terry Son and heir. Married with one son. Very charming but somewhat moody, either wildly idiotic or sombre. Dark hair, grey eyes. Marvellous writer of inspired nonsense. Over twenty-six years with Liebig Extract of Meat Co. Lives in Entre Rios, sixteen hours boat or train journey north-west.

Fred Dark, silent, medium height. Rather dumb, but a good chap. Employed with Liebig Extract's city office for last sixteen years.

Pat Perfectly adorable; very gay and generally vital. Has
(Mrs the dearest of husbands who thoroughly spoils her,
Angus) and two of the prettiest and most delightful children imaginable. Brown hair, lighter than ours, and brown eyes; very saucy. Is very popular and, being a lady of leisure, a real gadabout. Husband working directly under the British Admiralty here — and a very nice headache it is.

Jack The baby of the family. Nearly six foot, light-brown hair, blue-grey eyes. Very charming, but unreliable and inclined to be a bit self-indulgent . . . but of course we adore him. Commercial career somewhat chequered, but for last two years has been employed with the River Plate Coal Company selling anything from the proverbial peas, beans and nuts to sunflower and peanut cakes, and dried corn cobs. *C'est la guerre.*

Now, dear Uncle, I think I have written sufficient to give you a vague idea of your kindred under the Southern Cross . . . I don't know whether Dad has answered your last letter or not, but in any case he will reply sooner or later. Meanwhile, thank you again for your letter. We all hope by now you're quite your old self again, and send you our best love and wishes.

Your affectionate Niece,

Trilby.

Three dates are significant in Trilby's letter: 1894, the year of Trilby's birth; 1912, the year of grandmother Botley's death; and 1941, the year the letter was written.

Edward went to Argentina when Trilby was a baby, probably in 1895 or early 1896. His riding accident shortly after his arrival suggests he may have started work on a cattle ranch, but that is not necessarily so. He emigrated a decade after the waves of European immigrants invited to "people the desert" had subsided. By 1895 most of the immigrants were tradesmen, although in a few areas in the provinces of Santa Fé and Entre Rios agrarian colonisation had taken root. But by then, land which had been given freely had soared to a price beyond the means of most immigrants who, if they had no trade, were destined to tenant farming and share cropping at best, or hired occasional labour at worst.

One thing seems certain. Edward, at the age of thirty, married with two children, would have planned his emigration more meticulously than either of his brothers, Tom and Barney. Whatever he embarked on at first he must have felt confident that he could provide a home and livelihood to support his family when they joined him.

Edward and Carolyn had four children born in Argentina. When the youngest was still a baby, Carolyn and the children returned to England and remained there for eight years or so. They returned some time after Carolyn's mother's death in 1912 and before 1915 when Terry had already started work in Buenos Aires. There is no evidence that Edward left Argentina. Indeed, the fact that his family returned to the same house after eight years' absence is a good indication that he remained there.

There may have been some private reason for Carolyn to return to England, but the odds are that the move was politically rather than domestically motivated. In the first decade of the century there was much political turbulence and violence in Argentina, and Edward may have deemed it expedient for his wife and children to leave the country until things became calmer. They returned when Pat was ten years old, and although we have no record of her date of birth, it seems likely that their return would be in 1914, when the outbreak of the First World War was more significant than any civil disorder in Argentina.

Trilby writes that she became an "atheist" when she was fifteen; that was when she was living in England. Her long letter seems to have been sparked off by something Barney wrote to her, or contained in the poem he enclosed. Barney wrote poetry and, eventually, published his poems in a book entitled *Verse and Versus*. He may have intimated to Trilby that he had ceased to be a practising Catholic, but whatever chord he struck there is no evidence that he shared her belief in spiritualism. The prophetic death of Edward is interesting. He actually lived five years longer and died in 1946. Two of Edward's deceased brothers are mentioned by name in that context, and the Mary with the dress with the big flounces could be his sister Molly, who died in 1939, perhaps distinguishing herself from her twin sister by a particular dress she wore in their bygone Manchester days. The clairvoyance of Edward's children is also curiously interesting, not so much for its rarity, but for its occurrence in another grandchild of Paddy Finn. The daughter of Edward's brother Patrick, Florence, who remained a staunch Catholic for ninety-three years until her death in 1987 and showed no interest in the parapsychic, maintained that at times of deep family stress she would see her father at night standing at the foot of her bed dressed in military uniform. She spoke of it in such a matter of fact manner that one could not doubt her word.

Four months after Trilby wrote her letter to Barney the United States was at war. On Sunday, 7th December 1941, 360 Japanese war planes made a surprise attack at Pearl Harbor, Hawaii, sinking or seriously damaging five battleships, fourteen smaller ships, 200 aircraft and killing over 2,400 people. A few hours later Japan declared war on the United States.

On the following Thursday night the gasoline stove in Barney's home exploded and the house caught fire. Barney reckoned he could have smothered the flames if Henrietta had let him have a few blankets or rugs, but, as he put it, "she may have sensed how much worse it would have been to have lost her hubby at a time when she was no longer as young as she used to be and disengaged Irishmen were rare". That was the day that Germany and Italy declared war on the United States.

The homeless couple were given temporary shelter by a neighbour, and then Barney's printer, Harry Brown, offered them accommodation. Mrs Brown became sick soon after they arrived, and then a group of their daughters, one with her husband, came to stay. The refugees were then housed by a Mrs Carnaham, who gave them a warm welcome and then departed for Texas to stay with her son.

The fire occurred when their son Pat was in his final six months at college and money became a bit tight whilst the insurance claim was being sorted out. Lee came to the rescue with a loan for house repairs and Barney was able to provide Pat with the modest amount he needed to complete his studies.

Henrietta proudly went to Pat's graduation from the Colorado School of Mines. Unfortunately Barney was too busy with his newspaper to attend. The war was affecting life in Sarcoxie. Barney lost his linotype operator to the army. This time it was his daughter Margaret who came to the rescue.

Margaret and her husband, Clyde Moyer, had lived in Aruba ever since their marriage. Their son, William Finn Moyer (Bill), was born there on 24th November 1933 in Lago Colony Hospital, just outside the gate of the oil refinery. Bill's schooling in Aruba was interrupted when Margaret returned to Sarcoxie to operate Barney's linotype. Bill spent a school year during 1943-44 at Mexico Military Academy in Mexico, Missouri. After their return to Aruba, Bill resumed his education at Lagi High School and from there went to Cornell University, where he met his wife, Sue Sutton, of Garden City, New York. Bill and Sue were married in the Garden City Community Church on 25th November 1955.

On 21st January 1948, Barney and Henrietta had their golden wedding, and in that year their son Lee finally succeeded in persuading his father to write his autobiography.

Barney was prompted to begin this task by an illustrated article he had just read in *Life* magazine on the Irish poet and playwright, W. B. Yeats, and his native Sligo. There was a photograph of a mountain which reminded him of Kesh Corann, which lay east of the Clooneen farm where he was born. From there many a night Barney had seen as a small child the flitting lights on its hillside guiding the Little People in and out of its caves.

So at the age of seventy-nine Barney wrote his memoirs. He had spent three-quarters of his lifetime in America and had to rely on a long memory. In his later years he had dreamed of his birthplace many, many times. Once he woke up convinced he was there. It is not surprising therefore that the old craftsman penned a concise account of life at Clooneen as he saw it as a child, interlaced with Irish legends he had heard on Martin Millmow's knee. He summed up the history of his kinsfolk and the legends of Ireland in the lines of Lowell:

Barney Finn, as a retired newspaper editor, allowed to work in
Henrietta's garden.

Wondrous and awful are thy silent halls,
O, Kingdom of the past.
There lie bygone ages in their palls
Guarded by shadows past.

If childhood in Clooneen was a childhood dream his formative years in Manchester were a nightmare. He headed that part of his memoirs "Diarmuid". In Irish legend, Diarmuid was the trusted lieutenant of Finn McCool. Diarmuid had a magical mark on his chest which would make any woman who saw it fall in love with him. Finn McCool was engaged to Cormac MacCart's daughter, Grainne. As Diarmuid prepared for Finn's wedding he was seen by Grainne washing himself stripped to the waist. She saw the mark and immediately fell in love with him. They eloped and the enraged Finn McCool exiled Diarmuid.

So was Barney Finn exiled from his native Ireland through no fault of his own. Barney opens this episode of his life with the following paragraph:

"It was my misfortune to be made familiar with the grossest vice at an early age, beginning when I was in my eighth or ninth year and continuing until I stood at the gates of young manhood. It nauseated me. That, to some extent, explains how at the age of four score I am able to have sufficient good health to sit at a typewriter and record these experiences by thumping its keys with the 'hunt and peck' system."

To Barney, alcohol was the grossest vice. He had a repugnance to dwell upon his early years in Manchester. The Rising Sun is dismissed as being "in a slum area of the city, close to a gasworks". The four years until Paddy's death are almost bypassed. "The intevening time was one of such misery that I will have to omit most of the harrowing details from this account." The episodes of his life in Mancester that he put to paper are a precious account of life in those days. His omissions have made it difficult to retrace the family at that time.

Barney concluded his account of his life in Manchester with these words:

"But when I think of cities the gloomy, treeless, foggy, dirty, vice-ridden slums of Manchester come to mind, recalling the stench of it to my nostrils. I am thinking, of course, of the worst areas of the city in which it was my fate to spend my most easily impressed years. Parts of Manchester were quite as attractive as any other city in its class.

Such was the environment in which I moved through about fourteen years and was now about to leave. My young heart rejoiced in anticipation of adventures ahead, but I also had regrets because of sisters and friends, remaining thereabouts and touching close to poor human wretches, examples of what Robert Burns called man's inhumanity to man."

Unfortunately only small scraps of the twins' childhood in Manchester have been passed down through their children. Molly's daughter, Cecelia, said that the only home that her mother mentioned in Manchester was the one in Duke Street, which she described as "quite a nice street in those days". The twins' adventures at the Rising Sun were passed down by Roseanne to her daughter, Monica Duane. From Kate there was nothing. It was Patrick's daughter, Florence, who, when she was turned ninety, was able to recall life in Manchester in the closing years of the nineteenth century, but it was evident that she knew nothing about the happenings to the family there in the years before her mother brought her back from Malta after Patrick had died.

Barney's story from his embarkation on the *Servia* to the fire in his home in Sarcoxie in 1941 is the story of a man seeking his destiny in life and happily finding it. The American episode he entitled "The Greenhorn". He started as such, but had the strength and will to achieve his purpose. If Trilby found him diffident in his philosophy, perhaps this rhyme from his memoirs, recited in a speech made by the chairman of the examining committee of attorneys after Barney's admission to the Bar, sums it up robustly:

We come into this world naked and bare,
We go through the world laden with care,
We go out of the world God knows where,
But if we're thoro'breds here we'll be thoro'bred there.

Barney lived another seven years having not much else to do "other than sit by the lawn of evenings and watch a few dozen swifts descend into the Finn chimney". He died in Sarcoxie on 14th

October 1955 and is buried in the cemetery on the wide open plain outside Sarcoxie. Beside his grave are the graves of his wife, Henrietta, his daughter Margaret, and her husband Clyde Moyer.

And if the shades of Martin Millmow murmur through the leaves of the overhanging trees, "Here lies the greatest of the Finns", who is left to deny it?

Ireland Revisited

As far as is known, none of Paddy's children returned to Ireland to visit their birthplace. For the most part they had neither the time nor the means to make the journey worth while. It was left to their children and their grandchildren to seek out their roots there.

After Paddy left for England the property of the farmhouse at Clooneen passed to his brother Dominic, who had seven sons and a daughter named Mary Theresa. Mary Theresa married a local farmer named Joseph Doohan.

The last occupants of the farmhouse were Dominic's son Rob and his wife, Belinda Meehan. After they died the farm became the property of Kevin Doohan, the son of Joseph Doohan and Mary Theresa Finn. It was then that the living quarters were demolished and converted to cattle sheds.

The first of Paddy's descendants to visit Clooneen was the daughter of Molly Finn, Cecelia Harman. Cecelia was a school-teacher. In 1942 she left Coventry to become headmistress of St. Gregory's school, Stratford-upon-Avon. The following year she took a holiday in Ireland and called upon Rob and Belinda Finn at the Clooneen farm.

Cecelia retired in 1977 after twenty-five years at St. Gregory's. On her retirement, in appreciation of the contribution she made to the life of the parish, she received the Papal Bene Merente Award. After her retirement she travelled widely and made tours of the United States to visit members of the family there. She died on 24th November 1985, aged seventy-three.

Renewed interest in Clooneen began in America some years before Cecelia Harman's 1953 visit to Ireland, at the time when Barney Finn's son Pat attended the Colorado School of Mines. In 1939 Pat visited Colorado Springs and had a meal there with a man named James Francis Finn whose family came from the Clooneen area. Pat asked Jimmy Finn to draw him a map of the area to send to Barney. Jimmy obliged by scrawling a rough sketch on a paper serviette. The map located Clooneen just north of Gorteen in the area east of the Gorteen to Ballymote road and west of the Owenmore river. When Barney received the map from Pat he added a few comments and sent it to Edward in Buenos Aires. Edward returned the map with some additions which included O'Gorman's public house in Gorteen, the cairn on the summit of Kesh and the raths where he almost met his death as a young boy when his brother Michael's revolver accidentally fired. The completed map located Paddy Finn's farm about halfway between the Ballymote road and the Owenmore and Jack Finn's farm to its south over the hill. Off the map Edward had marked to the north Rosses Point where a Mr Finn had met an untimely end shortly before their mother died.

Thirty years and more passed before Pat Finn had the opportunity of exploring the territory encompassed within Jimmy Finn's serviette. His work as a petroleum engineer and geologist involved frequent journeys to the Middle East. On one of his trips he arranged that he and his wife, Irene, should take a short break in Ireland. They hired a car, drove up to Gorteen and, with much difficulty and scratching of the car, drove down the muddy lane leading to the farm where his father was born.

The farm was deserted. Belinda Finn, the farm's last occupant, had died in 1969 and was buried with her husband Rob at Kilshalvey. After tramping around in the mud and surveying a scene that had changed little since Barney's childhood, they drove back to Gorteen where they met Mick Finn of Ragwood, who worked at the creamery at the Boyle road intersection.

Mick took them to Ragwood where Paddy's son John had died of fever after being invalided home from Malta. At Mick's home they met his wife Kathy. After trying to unravel the threads of family history for a while from the days of the great potato famine when Jack Finn brought his family over the border from County Mayo, Mick stood up and announced, "Now you should see where your father's father came from."

They got into the car and Mick directed them to Jack Finn's farm in Cloontia, where Paddy was born. There they met its occupants, Pat and Annie Finn. The small farm was the beginning of the known history of the Finn family. Here time had almost stood still for nearly two centuries whilst generations of emigrant Finns had been caught up and whirled around in the rapids of progress.

Pat and Irene drove south to Shannon and back to a life far removed from the one they had just left. They had thoroughly enjoyed their visit and the hospitality and friendliness Pat's kinfolk had shown them.

Lee Finn's younger daughter, Margaret Finn Harding, made an exploratory trip to Ireland and unearthed some Finn history among the Sligo registry records, but it was her cousin, Bill Moyer, who delved the deepest. Bill is the genealogist of the family and has spent many long hours of painstaking research of the Finn family. For many years he worked in personal investment counselling with the United States Trust Company of New York in Wall Street. His work took him to London and Dublin to meet clients and gave him the opportunity to visit County Sligo.

When Bill Moyer made his first visit to Ireland he did not know that his uncle Pat had already been there, and was unaware of the exact location of Paddy's farm. Clooneen is not marked on a road map and he missed it as he drove north through County Sligo to Ballymote. He caught sight of Kesh as it stood out majestically above the gently rolling countryside, and stopped now and again to squelch around rain-soaked grassy cemeteries and noted the names of Finn, Hannon, Kane and Millmoe carved on the mossy Celtic crosses. He spent the night in a motel in the town of Sligo, and next morning drove up the hill to the new municipal building where he spent two hours examining the birth and death records.

He quickly found his grandfather's record of birth: 7th March 1869, father Pat Finn, parish Clooneen, mother Mary Hannon, father's trade farmer. That was in Book 3. In Book 1 the date of birth of Edward Finn was recorded as 14th May 1865 and in Book 5 the twins, Maria Finn and Rose Ann Finn, born on 1st June 1872.

Edward was the first of Paddy's children to appear in the registry of births. Dates of births prior to 1864 are conjectural. In many cases the year of birth is calculated by subtracting the age shown on a death certificate from the date of death, but this can be wildly misleading. In so many cases the witnesses to death have no idea of the age of the deceased person. In the case of Paddy Finn, for instance, the death certificate gives his age as sixty, the burial records as fifty, whereas Bernard believed his father was aged forty-six when he died. Bernard's estimate has been accepted as the most likely in the calculation of Paddy's year of birth. In the cases of the children older than Edward, the years of birth of Tom and

Kate have been calculated from their ages recorded in the Manchester census of 1881, supplemented in the case of Kate by the age shown on her marriage certificate. As James and Patrick do not appear in the Manchester census their years of birth have been reckoned as being between 1861, the calculated year of Kate's birth, and 1865, the recorded year of Edward's birth. John's year of birth is calculated from the entry in the Gorteen register of deaths: 22nd September 1876, Clooneen, John Finn, bachelor, age 22, farmer's son, fever 3 weeks, Pat Finn informant, present at death, Ragwood.

Bill Moyer found other family names in the death registers. On page 98 of Book 3 is Paddy's wife, Mary Finn, died of fever at Clooneen on 4th December 1876, aged forty. In the same book on page 61 is the death of Paddy's father, Jack Finn, of cancer on 5th October 1877, at the age of eighty-one. There is good reason to suppose that the year of death has been entered incorrectly, and that he died in 1875. The record is thirty pages before the record of John's death in September 1876 and thirty-seven pages before Mary's death. If Jack Finn was aged eight-one when he died in 1875 he would be born about 1794. The death of his widow Catherine is recorded on page 100 of Book 7. She died of old age on 7th January 1894. Her age is given as eighty, in which case she would have been born in 1814 and would be twenty years younger than her husband. It seems far more likely that she was near to ninety when she died. Her death was reported by Paddy's brother Thomas, and she died at his home in Kiltycreen.

From the entries noted in the records it is interesting to speculate on interrelationships among the Finn and Hannon families.

In the death records there are two Mary Finns apart from Paddy's wife. The first Mary Finn was a farmer's widow who died at Bucklame in November 1872 at the reported age of seventy-two. The death was reported by Maurice Hannon. He also reported the death of Maurice Hannon who died at Bucklame in February 1868 at the reported age of eighty, presumably his father. If this Mary Finn was the sister of Maurice Hannon, then clearly Paddy's wife Mary was not.

The second Mary Finn died at Annaghmore in December 1885 at the reported age of ninety. She was the widow of Tom Finn, farmer, and her death was reported by her son Luke. Tom Finn would be a contemporary of Jack Finn, and could possibly be his brother. What is certain is that Luke Finn was not Paddy's brother.

Among the death records there is the possibility of discovering the mother of Paddy's wife Mary, who from her death record would be born in 1836.

The first entrant to qualify by age is Bridget Hannon who died a widow in April 1869 at Monasteriden at the reported age of sixty. The claim of Bridget Hannon to be Mary's mother is supported by a curious gaffe in Barney Finn's memoirs where he writes, "our place was called Clooneen, which I have lately been told means a small monastery". Could it be that Barney had confused Clooneen with his mother's birthplace Monasteriden? The gaffe is not conclusive but is highly indicative.

Two married women who qualify by age died in 1869 at the age of sixty-five. In each case it is likely that the husband reported the death. The first is Mary Hannon of Cloonsilla, whose death was reported by Paddy Hannon. The second is Catherine Hannon of Bucklame, death reported by John Hannon.

The last entrant is Nelly Hannon of Greyfield, who died a widow in September 1870 at the reported age of sixty. Greyfield is just across the river from Paddy's farm and it is tempting to think that that is where he met his wife and where two brothers lived.

There is, however, one possibility to consider. Paddy may have worked for Flannery of Ballaghaderreen before he was married, in which case his journey to work would take him through both Cloonsilla and Monasteriden. Cloonsilla is on the Ballaghaderreen road between Ragwood and Monasteriden. Monasteriden is only a mile or so from Ballaghaderreen, just west of Lough Gara.

Among all these options of Paddy's wife's parentage the most significant clue stems from Barney Finn's reference to the "small monastery", indicating that Mary Finn's mother was Bridget Hannon of Monasteriden.

Bill Moyer finished his search of Sligo records at noon in the hope of finding Paddy's farm before driving down to Dublin for a business appointment that evening. But he had little time to spare. At the Gorteen crossroads he was told that Clooneen was the name given to the crossroads he had passed just north of the town. He drove back, turned east at the crossroads down a country lane that crossed the Owenmore over a little bridge, then went up a hill where he found a farm. But the farm was not Paddy's. Its occupant sent her small daughters to fetch a man working in the fields. The man left his work without hesitation, and although he did not know any

Finns, he was very friendly and helpful. He pointed to a hill to the south-west that used to be called "Paddy Finn's hill". He said the man who owned it now was Kevin Doohan who he believed was related to the Finns. He indicated some houses in the distance as being Greyfield.

There was no time to pursue the search for the farm. Bill headed for the road to Dublin. Somewhere to the east of Boyle he stopped the car at a sign pointing up a steep hill to a "Megalithic Tomb". He climbed a narrow path to the top of the hill where he saw several large crude rock slabs standing erect and balancing a flat one on top. As he stood there the sun came out from behind the clouds, lighting up the beautiful emerald green countryside below for miles around. There was a smell of peat smoke in the air. This was the Ireland his grandfather knew as a child, and his father, and his father into the dim, unknown past.

On the way back to the car he picked some raspberries growing wild by the hedgerow. They tasted delicious. He had not eaten or drunk since breakfast. He sped on to Dublin for a thoroughly enjoyable dinner of broiled salmon washed down with Smithwick's Irish beer, after which he felt extremely fortunate to have found his way back to his grandfather's native land.

The next morning he had some time to spare and wandered round to the Genealogical Office at Dublin Castle where he made notes of entries in *Griffith's Valuation of Tenements and Tithe Applotments* for the parish of Kilfree, Union of Boyle, County Sligo, years 1835 to 1858. There he found Jack Finn's farm and three parcels of land totalling seventy-one acres leased from Edward J. Cooper, Paddy's farm with twenty-six acres of land leased from Miss Sallie Powell, ten acres of bogland shared by Paddy and his father, and a further ten acres of bog shared by them and Thomas Duffy, all leased from Edward Cooper. The last parcel of land leased to Jack Finn consists of a house and twenty-six acres. This could be the farm he leased for Paddy. The house and land leased by Paddy from Sallie Power could have provided the home of Martin Millmow, who Barney believed was his father's tenant. Michael Finn's farm at Ragwood was also identified. For the rest there were Finns and Hannons all over the place who may or may not have been Paddy's relatives.

With some time to spare Bill crossed Dublin and called at the Ordnance Survey Office to learn something about the territorial divisions of the country and the derivation of Irish place names.

Ireland has four main territorial divisions, the provinces of Connaught, Leinster, Munster and Ulster. Each province is divided into counties. Six of the eight counties of Ulster remain in the United Kingdom as Northern Ireland. Its other two counties and the three other provinces form the Republic of Ireland. Within the counties there are 325 historic baronies. Under the Poor Law Relief Act of 1838 small districts or Unions were made responsible for the care of all paupers in their area. The Union was an amalgam of civil parishes, and each parish was an amalgam of townlands. Within the townland there were placenames, such as Clooneen, which could denote an area within the bounds of a small farm or two. The location of Clooneen is in the townland of Riverstown (or Riversdale) in Kilfree Parish, Union of Boyle, Barony of Coolavin, County Sligo, Connaught.

Irish placenames are anglicised forms of Irish Gaelic from which their meaning can be derived. There is no letter 'k' in the Gaelic alphabet and the innumerable names beginning with 'K' are anglicised form of the original Gaelic. Names beginning with Kil relate to the Irish Gaelic *cill*, meaning burial place. The remainder of the name is usually the name of a saint. Thus Kilfree becomes Cillfraoich, the burial place of St. Fraochan. As the local church is generally named after the saint, *cill* is often interpreted as church, but this meaning of *cill* is strictly confined to the Gaelic of the Scottish Highlands.

Clooneen is derived from the Gaelic *cluain*, meaning meadow. It is sometimes referred to as Clooneenbaun from *cluainban*, white meadow. The Owenmore comes from *abhainnmor*, great river. Ragwood is curious. The name seems to be derived from the English translation of the anglicised version of the Gaelic — if that does not sound too Irish. Another name for Ragwood is Kilstraghlan, which is suspiciously like the Gaelic *coillstreach-lanach*, meaning straggling wood.

Bill Moyer completed his business in Dublin and returned to New York well pleased with his visit. Although it had been frustrating not to have found Clooneen he had gleaned some useful information about the Finn family and the county in which they lived. He had walked in their townland and had experienced the warmth and friendliness of its people. There may be another opportunity to discover Clooneen.

When his uncle Pat learned of the trouble Bill had in locating

Clooneen, he proposed a joint expedition. At that time Pat Finn was in charge of some oil drilling platforms in the Red Sea and went there regularly for a month at a time. He suggested that if Bill happened to make another business trip across the Atlantic they might be able to meet up in Ireland.

The occasion at last arose, and with some personal inconvenience to both uncle and nephew a meeting was arranged in Ireland. Bill arrived first. His plane touched down at dawn, and as Pat's plane was not due to arrive until ten o'clock that evening, he hired a car and set off for County Sligo. He reached Gorteen just after noon and began his exploration with an abortive attempt to climb the hill of Kilshavy just west of Clooneen to explore the cemetery there. The climb was not a success. He got caught in the hawthorn bushes on the hill slopes and was bitten by a dog. To add to his discomfiture the threatening clouds released a deluge of rain. As he slithered down the hillside he met the owner of the dog, Francis Meehan, a relative of Belinda Meehan who had married Rob Finn, the last occupant of Paddy's farm. Francis told him an easier way to reach the cemetery on top of the hill, but he thought it unlikely that any of Bill's relatives were buried there. He thought it more probable that they were buried at Mount Irwin, near Knocknaskeagh, in Gaelic, *Cnocnaseuch*, the hill of the hawthorn bushes. Bill decided he would postpone the climb up Kilshavy hill until the following day. He gave a cheery farewell to Francis Meehan and his zealous sheepdog and set out to walk to Clooneen following Pat Finn's written directions.

There was a new house on the Gorteen road where the mud path to Paddy's farm sloped down to the east. Its owner, Don Conlon, came out and confirmed that Bill had found the right path. Bill climbed the fence and squelched down the path's muddy slope. About five hundred yards along the path he found the farmhouse and its sheds. The buildings were in a rundown condition after being unoccupied for many years except by cattle whose hooves and droppings had churned the approach road and field entrances into puddles of mud. To the east of the farm the valley of Clooneen opened out into a flat plain bordering the Owenmore river as it flowed in a curve from south to north-east. Across the valley to the north Bill could see a hill surmounted by two circular raths about fifty feet apart. He left the deserted farmhouse and the outsheds filled with cattle sheltering from the rain and climbed the hill to get a better look at the raths.

A view of Clooneen from the south.

The raths were not very large, only about thirty feet in diameter. Their broken walls were patched with earth and rock. If these were truly prehistoric hill forts there would be cold comfort for the garrison on that rainswept hill. Bill climbed among brambles and hawthorns up to the ridge of the hill to get a better look at Kesh to the north-east. Three horses standing in earth-banked, water-ditched enclosures stared at him as he passed. The rain came down incessantly, making the soggy ground treacherous under foot. The descent was a slither in the direction of the Owenmore.

Rather surprisingly the ground was much firmer by the river. Bill walked along its bank surefooted back towards Clooneen. Beside him the stream ran fast and clear through the dark green meadow. As he neared the farm, Bill looked out for the blackthorn that had been Michael's tree, but he could not see it.

He squelched along the muddy path leading to the Gorteen road, then stopped to take stock of his appearance. His clothing was soaked with rain, his shoes were caked in mud, and there was a jagged tear in his slacks where Francis Meehan's sheepdog had taken a friendly bite. He had been invited to have afternoon tea at the Conlons, and soon decided he was not fit to cross anybody's threshold. Nevertheless he went and was made welcome.

There was a peat fire burning in the living-room hearth around which four red-cheeked children were playing. There was another visitor there, Don Conlon's mother. Bill chatted to her as he thankfully drank a hot cup of tea and ate Irish soda bread and currant jam in the warmth of the fire. When he discovered that her maiden name was Carberry he enquired about John Carberry and his National School which was responsible for his grandfather's elementary education. She confirmed that the school was north of Clooneen in the Tunnagh townland. In 1881 a new school was built just south of the Conlons' home. John Carberry was headmaster and lived next to the school. Now both school and headmaster's house were in ruins. To learn more of his family's history the Conlons suggested that Bill should have a talk with Kevin Doohan, a grandson of Dominic Finn. Kevin's father, Joseph Doohan, married Dominic's daughter, Mary Theresa Finn. Kevin became the owner of Paddy's farm after Rob and Belinda Finn died.

The Conlons told Bill how to find Kevin Doohan's home at Rathbaun on the Tobercurry road, but the day was far spent. It was still raining hard and he had to drive for several hours to Shannon airport to meet Pat Finn who was arriving from Egypt. As he drove through Galway he met a rainstorm. To add to his troubles there was a sports car rally on the road that evening and he was relieved to reach Shannon in one piece. The airport was almost deserted, but the small restaurant was still open. He ate and then slept at the motel until ten o'clock when Pat's plane was due. The Dublin plane was late and it was approaching midnight before Bill and Pat met. Both were thoroughly tired. They made brief plans for the morrow before bedding down to a welcome night's sleep.

The next morning they headed for County Sligo. It was still raining. They stopped at the creamery in Gorteen to see Mick Finn, whom Pat had met on his previous visit, but Mick was at home. At Ragwood Mick and his wife Kathy gave them a warm welcome. Kathy made tea for Bill and Mick, and gave Pat a good measure of poteen, whilst their son Pat attended to the turf fire.

Mick told Bill that he was born in 1904. His father, also named Michael, was born in 1845 and died in 1930. He had two brothers named Edward and Thomas. His grandfather, another Michael, came from Cloontia and had married Kitty Radican of Ragwood, whose father gave them some land there as a dowry. This Michael Finn was clearly Jack Finn's son and Paddy Finn's brother.

They asked Mick if it were likely that their kinsfolk were buried at Kilshalvy, but he agreed with Frank Meehan that the Clooneen Finns were buried at Mount Irwin, about half a mile west of Clooneen by Knocknaskeagh.

They found the cemetery near the ruins of a church in a little valley south of the Tobercurry road. They found the graves of several Finns and Hannons, but could not see Mary's grave. As they searched they reflected it was almost the centenary of Mary's death. If her grave were here Paddy would have come here to say a last farewell before he left for England. It seemed fitting that her grandson and great-grandson should return a century later to pay their respects.

From the cemetery they headed for the Tobercurry road to Kevin Doohan's farm about a mile to the north. The two-storey farmhouse stood just off the road. Two young men were in the farmyard. They introduced themselves as Kevin's sons, Joseph and Jeremy. As they were speaking, Kevin came striding down the hill from the barn to see what the strangers wanted. He was a dark-haired, serious-looking man in his mid-forties with long sideburns growing down his cheeks. When Pat and Bill explained who they were and why they were interested in Clooneen he confirmed that Dominic Finn was his grandfather and believed it correct that Dominic and James had taken over the farm there from their brother Patrick.

Kevin's mother was Mary Theresa Finn, Dominic Finn's daughter, who had married Joseph Doohan, Kevin's father. Kevin thought that the Finns originally came from Leinster or Limerick but were driven from their farms by the Cromwellian Act of Settlement and sought refuge in Connaught, but this was a historic possibility rather than known family history, which begins with Jack Finn's farm in Cloontia.

Kevin showed Pat and Bill the large rath on the hill above his farm. Within the rath there is a deep cavern from which, it is said, a buried tunnel, or souterrain, extends across the valley to souterrains buried in the hill opposite.

Bill made some enquiries about the Clooneen farm from its new owner, Kevin's son Joseph. Dominic had made extensions and alterations to Paddy's farm. The original house and fireplace were in the centre of the building and had now been demolished, leaving only a roofed outer wall to serve as a cowshed. And the blackthorn which Michael claimed proprietary as a hide?

Somewhat startled by the question Joseph Doohan replied, "I

rooted it out just about two years ago. It was called Michael's bush. Years ago, when the water used to flood almost to the house, it would be out in the water. Michael hollowed it out so that he could sit inside and shoot the ducks."

It is not given to many to be remembered a hundred years later by the name of the tree they climbed as a boy.

As for the curlews and corncrakes that Barney remembered as a young child, Kevin said that curlews were still to be found occasionally. Corncrakes seem to have left the area, although when he was a boy there were times when he could hardly sleep because of the noise they made at night. Joseph added that he had heard one two years ago. They nest in fields of grain, and in the old times the harvester would make a detour round their nesting places. Modern machinery is not so discriminatory and the nesting ground has been destroyed.

It was starting to get dark when Pat and Bill left Rathbaun. They drove north through the town of Sligo to a hotel on the peninsula named Rosses Point. The next morning they drove south and examined Kesh. They could see the caves in the limestone outcrop high up the hillside. Cattle were grazing on the slopes below them, so access to them could not be too difficult. It occurred to Bill that if farmers used to climb the slopes in the evening to bring home their cattle their lanterns could be the fairy lights that his grandfather saw from his bedroom at Clooneen.

Bill wanted to climb Kesh to get a close look at the cairn, which on a clear day could be seen for miles around looking like a miniature hill at one end of its broad, flat summit, but was deterred somewhat by a delightful old lady they met whilst searching for a path to begin the ascent. She warned them that it would be a hard and slippery climb, and possibly dangerous too now that the mists were beginning to enshroud the summit. Besides, she added, the cairn was only a pile of ordinary rocks, hardly worth the effort. She told them that the cairn marked the burial ground of Queen Maev, whose husband, King Olliol Olum, was buried at Knocknarea near Sligo.

They drove round Kesh seeking a route to the summit, but the mist had thickened and blanketed the upper slopes. They abandoned the climb and headed for Ballymote en route for Clooneen. At Kilshalvy they chanced to see Francis Meehan walking along the road with his dog. They stopped the car and

Francis got in to guide them to the cemetery in the hope of finding the grave of Mary Finn there. As they walked up the hill to the cemetery, Francis repeated his conviction that the Finn burial ground was at Mount Irwin, although his father's sister Belinda and her husband Rob Finn, son of Dominic Finn, were buried here at Kilshalvy. He corroborated known family history by saying that Dominic's father was Jack Finn, originally from Cloontia, and extended it by saying that Dominic married Anne McDermot Roe from Ballinafad. They had seven sons: Paddy, Thomas Joseph, John Henry, George, Jimmy, Benedict Simon, and Rob.

They searched the cemetery in vain. The old gravestones were worn and mostly illegible. They found the ruins of an abbey, a large Celtic cross, and many hummocks and sunken spots in the grass marking long-forgotten graves. Headstones were few, and mostly illegible. None bore the name of Finn.

The time had come for the two travellers to press on to Cloontia, although they were forewarned that Ann Finn had died since Pat's first visit and that her husband Pat had taken to spending most of his time "in town", meaning in the pub.

At a small crossroads they found Cloontia. It consisted of a general store, a pub and two or three houses. They stopped at the pub and were given directions to Pat Finn's farm, a mile or so to the east. They found it by a little stream. To the north-east Kesh was clearly visible across the plain. They prowled round the farm, but its owner was neither at home nor in the Cloontia pub they had just left.

It had been a long, tiring day. They drove back to Shannon and had an excellent steak dinner and a good night's sleep to fortify themselves for their final day in Ireland.

The next morning Pat busied himself making his airline reservations at Shannon airport whilst Bill drove into Limerick. In Limerick library he found a census of Ireland dating from Cromwellian times. The only Finns he could find were in Cork County, Barony of Ibawne and Barymore, where he discovered ten O'Finns and twelve McFinns. But there were nine families named Hannin in Roscommon County, and in County Antrim eight families named Hannon. The name Kane was not to be found, but as the Irish Gaelic does not contain the letter 'k' the Kanes, and also the Keanes, could be the anglicised version of an earlier name. Although the information from the Limerick library was skimpy it lended support to Kevin Doohan's belief that the ancestors of Jack Finn originally came from outside Connaught.

The expedition was over. That afternoon Pat flew from Shannon on his journey home to Corpus Christi, Texas, and Bill flew to London to meet a client that evening. The mission had been worth while. In Ireland they had felt close to Barney and his family. There the pace of life had dealt kindly with the memories of Paddy and his children. The day had not yet come when all memory had been obliterated. One day in the unknown future that day will come, and it will seem that they never lived.

But they did.